PERSPECTIVES IN SCIENCE & THOUGHT

Let Us
REASON

A COLLECTION OF SHORT CLASSICS

DOES HE WHO THINKS HAVE TO BELIEVE?

WHY DOES GOD ALLOW IT?

IS THIS A GOD OF LOVE?

Dr. A.E. Wilder-Smith

D1293720

THE WORD
FOR TODAY

P.O. Box 8000, Costa Mesa, CA 92628 • Web Site: www.twft.com • E-mail: info@twft.com

Let Us Reason
by A.E. Wilder-Smith

© 2007 The Word For Today

P.O. Box 8000, Costa Mesa, CA 92628
(800) 272-WORD (9673)
Web Site: www.twft.com
E-mail: info@twft.com

ISBN: 978-1-59751-037-0

Does He Who Thinks Have To Believe?
by Dr. A.E. Wilder-Smith
First printing, 1981

Is This A God Of Love?
by Dr. A.E. Wilder-Smith
First printing, 1991, translated from the original German
by Petra Wilder-Smith

Why Does God Allow It?
by Dr. A.E. Wilder-Smith
First printing, 1980

FOREWORD

Most creationists look back to the publication of *The Genesis Flood* in 1961 as the event which catalyzed the modern creation movement. It was written by my father, Dr. Henry Morris, a scientist, and Dr. John Whitcomb, a theologian, and presented a firm case for the biblical view of true history. I was a teenager in the home in the late 50s when the manuscript was in preparation, and knew that worldwide, few Christians with scientific training would even consent to look at the manuscript. Creation was a dead subject, and even biblical inerrancy was in disfavor as long as Genesis couldn't be defended.

One of those early scientists who helped review the manuscript and stand up for creation and biblical inerrancy was the learned Swiss scientist, Dr. A.E. Wilder-Smith. It was not a position to be assumed by the faint hearted, and yet he maintained a valiant crusade for truth. Within a few years books and pamphlets began flowing from his pen, presenting creation thinking to the European continent. Within a few more years his influence had extended to the New World as well. The film series "How the World Came to be," first produced in the Netherlands and then recast in many languages, introduced this winsome and eloquent spokesman to millions.

And what a spokesman he was! With three earned doctorates and an international reputation in scientific and governmental circles he represented his field and his Lord well. Impeccable science coupled with careful biblical scholarship provided a platform which yielded much fruit. Truly he earned the reputation as one of the founders of today's thriving creation movement.

LET US REASON

His writings and lectures were marked with original research and clear thinking which helped placed creation on firm footing. He specialized on intelligent design concepts and information theory, both death blows to wishful evolutionary thoughts of origin by random mutation and natural selection. Evolution is a view of history more than a scientific hypothesis, and as such can't be proven or disproven in a strict scientific sense, but his cleverly-framed arguments came close. Only a willingly ignorant (2 Peter 3:5) mind could ignore his logic.

But such is the state of the unbelieving world today. Many look directly at clear evidence and choose not to see. This collection of Wilder-Smith's writings will present that evidence in his engaging style and with such great power that an open mind must deal with it. Each of his books has had a lasting ministry, but their sphere of influence deserves to be widened. In the lives and education of most, this evidence has always been censored, but no longer. Christians will once again be thrilled to see how well the biblical worldview handles the evidence. Seekers will find the goal of their quest. Skeptics will be confronted with the "rightness" of the position.

I thank God for "gifting" this world with Dr. A.E. Wilder-Smith, a true warrior for the faith. Even though he has left this life, I pray his ministry perseveres through his writings and bears much fruit, which will itself persevere throughout eternity.

—Dr. John D. Morris, Ph.D.
President of Institute for Creation
Research
www.icr.org

PREFACE

It is my pleasure and honor to introduce this new edition of some of Arthur Ernest Wilder-Smith's most popular books: *Does He Who Thinks Have to Believe? Is this a God of Love?* and *Why does God Allow it?* These books are intended for all inquiring minds including scientists, non-scientists, and students, who concern themselves with the fundamental questions of life.

Allow me to briefly recapitulate some essential facts about the late well-known, prolific English scientist and author affectionately known as A.E. or A.E.W.S. Besides his numerous scientific publications, Professor Wilder-Smith authored a wide range of books that have retained their relevance and provocativeness.

As a young student Arthur was an atheist, molded by his education in an English boarding school and at Oxford University. His professors at Oxford, such as Sir Gavin de Beer, a prominent atheist and Darwinist, Sir Robert Robinson, and E. B. Ford, were brilliant scientists who greatly influenced Arthur. Professor de Beer's first-class lectures in evolution and zoology fascinated him immensely. A young and impressionable student, Arthur appropriated many of his professors' scientific arguments and used them to justify and defend his own atheism. In addition, his personal observation of the numerous injustices of daily life convinced Arthur against the existence of God. "If a loving God really existed, He surely would not have tolerated all the injustice and suffering evident in the world," he concluded.

LET US REASON

During the great depression of the 1930s, Arthur and his family of farmers experienced a raging conflict over a tax imposed upon the farming population. The law mandated landowners to pay a large annual tax (called a "tithe") to the State Anglican Church. The "tithe" was to be paid even by farmers who did not belong to the church or were atheists. The impoverished landowners already had great difficulty sustaining their own families and paying the wages of their farm hands. Thus, many farmers refused to pay this unjust tax. To make matters worse, this conflict was fuelled by the fact that many ministers were perceived to not believe or live by what they were paid to preach. This, of course, led to much resentment toward the church.

Having lived through such severe injustice, Arthur consequently decided that the church was for the most part humbug and Christian teaching hypocrisy. He considered himself to be an atheist, a position he believed at the time to be confirmed by science. Arthur was disillusioned with life despite his success in his studies and academic career. Life was irrational and cruel. He had also confused religiosity with Christianity. Arthur dealt with this and other existential and controversial faith issues in his book, *Is This a God of Love?* He could not believe in a loving God on account of all the bitter injustice in the world.

In his quest, Wilder-Smith researched and discussed the existential questions of life with a broad range of friends, including academicians and intellectuals. He appreciated the importance of understanding these issues for one's life and destiny. It was during this period of his life that he made several life-changing acquaintances, the most significant of whom was General Frost. The youngest general in the British Armed Forces, Frost had an outstanding personality. And he was also a devout Christian who strongly challenged Arthur's atheistic beliefs. Their interaction eventually led to Arthur's conversion to a personal faith in Jesus Christ.

Continuing his academic pursuits at Oxford University, Arthur made another significant acquaintance. The well-known professor, C.S. Lewis, became his examiner of general knowledge. C.S. Lewis' superb lectures and books deeply impressed and greatly influenced Arthur's intellectual life and thinking. For many years, he committed himself to finding scientific answers to the genesis of life, the origin of genetic information and man.

As a result of his own intensive scientific investigation, he came to the firm acknowledgment that life could not have originated through random self-organization. One needed to postulate some kind of super-intelligence — a Creator — behind life and creation. This recognition led to intense scientific scrutiny and rejection of Darwinism. For decades Dr. Wilder-Smith engaged in successful yet tough public debates and lectures around the world. He wrote many books that are a synopsis of the arguments and analyses he developed over the years. Some of the books he has written are: *The Creation of Life, Man's Origins, Man's Destiny, The Natural Sciences Know Nothing of Evolution,* and *The Time Dimension.* They were written to assist others who find themselves in the same battles Arthur fought when he came to believe in a Creator and then a personal Savior.

His struggles, his inquiring scientific approach to issues, his interaction with strong thinkers and personalities, and his deep faith shaped him into a leader with compassion and deep understanding of life's existential questions.

LET US REASON

It was my husband's greatest joy to share the fruit of his own growth and walk in faith with others. His ardent desire was to better equip Christians for the spiritual battle, a desire further realized in the publishing of this new edition of his books.

As a scientist and professor of pharmacology in many universities and countries, Dr. Wilder-Smith was active in diverse areas of expertise. His work included research in cancer, leprosy, tuberculosis, diabetes, and organic chemistry. He was a beloved father, husband, and teacher.

— Beate Wilder-Smith

ACKNOWLEDGMENTS

First of all, I want to extend my thanks to our beloved and greatly esteemed Pastor Chuck Smith of Calvary Chapel Costa Mesa, who for many years has been a loyal friend and supporter. Without his encouragement and support, this edition and previous works would never have been realized. Special thanks also go to *The Word For Today Publishers* with its efficient and caring team. Lastly, I am grateful to our children for their steadfast support and advice over the years.

— Beate Wilder-Smith

BOOK ONE

Does He Who Thinks Have to Believe?

By A.E. Wilder-Smith

Contents

CHAPTER

1

Thoughts and Beliefs of the Neanderthalers

A Neanderthaler, living in a small tribe isolated from present-day civilization in the forests of Papua, knew nothing of modern man and modern civilization. Our technological way of life with its radios, television, telephones, and automobiles was unknown to him. He did not even know what a machine was. He lived in a pure stone-age culture. Yet his thoughts were by no means primitive, for his knowledge of botany and the healing powers of various plants was extensive. Thus although he knew nothing of airplanes, his knowledge of pharmacognosy—the healing powers of plants—was far greater than ours. He was also quite well educated in certain aspects of art, for he had visited some of the caves higher up in the forests. There he had learned how Cro-Magnon man painted beautiful scenes on the walls of these dark caves. With simple colors he quite artistically portrayed animals and plants. He had also mastered the art of drawing on bones. He really loved all aspects of nature and knew how to treat its plants and animals.

This small Neanderthal tribe lived together peacefully and happily in complete isolation.

One fine day our Neanderthaler leader saw something in the sky that terrified him. He had no idea what it could be and therefore was very frightened. We, in his place, would have recognized the sound of a low flying jumbo jet, which was approaching him at great speed and low altitude. The machine left a long trail of black smoke in its wake which was preceded by a long, dark red burst of flame. The jumbo jet was rapidly losing altitude despite its increasing speed and erratic flight course; it seemed to be aiming directly for him, so the Neanderthaler hastily fled into a nearby cave far below the earth's surface.

Shortly afterwards there was a terrible ear-shattering noise close by: trees were flattened, metal and wood crashed to the ground. Then suddenly it was uncannily quiet. Only the faint hiss and crackle of a small forest fire could be heard. The Neanderthaler waited for a few minutes, then very cautiously he crept forth from his hiding place and fearfully surveyed his surroundings. He perceived the burning remains of the huge machine that had crashed. As it crashed, the machine had exploded and razed many trees before coming to a halt. Its cargo lay scattered everywhere. Crates had been broken open by the impact of the crash. The wreck was surrounded by radios, television sets, telephones, and car engines. The half-burned remains of the crew were a hideous sight. The partly charred and terribly disfigured corpses were almost unrecognizable, although our Neanderthaler recognized them immediately as corpses of his own kind. They were, of course, the remains of modern men, *Homines sapientes sapientes.*

With great caution he approached this terrible scene. Several small fires flickered feebly before dying out completely. Everything became very quiet—the corpses lay silent in all sorts of possible and impossible positions around the wreck. Obviously all the passengers were dead. Frightened and deeply shocked, our Neanderthaler surveyed the scene of this catastrophe. Naturally he felt helpless. What could a helpless, even though intelligent, Neanderthaler do in this situation? Being a sensible Neanderthaler, he first fetched his wife, who sent the children away and forbade them to follow her. Then Mr. and Mrs. Neanderthaler ran to the wreck with all its terrible secrets. Having respectfully examined it all, they fetched their children to the wreck. Having prepared them appropriately, they shared with them this mysterious, terrible incident.

The children, once they had recovered a little from the shock of seeing this catastrophe, began to examine the Jumbo's scattered cargo. Crates, some burst open, were scattered everywhere—typewriters (it was an export shipment), radios, TVs, and spare parts were to be found in vast amounts in the proximity of the wreck. The function of these machines puzzled the Neanderthalers. In a large, almost undamaged crate the children found a Japanese jeep, which was even in good working order. Inside the jeep lay all the necessary tools for the repair and maintenance of the vehicle. Just like our children, Neanderthal children were inquisitive, as well as quick. Once they had overcome their initial fears, the children's curiosity prevailed.

WHAT THE NEANDERTHALERS LEARNED

Very quickly the Neanderthal children had discovered how to remove and replace the jeep's wheels. The functions of the various controls were also quickly established. To their great delight, they found that turning a certain key would start up the engine. Pressing a certain pedal increased the engine speed — which could be decreased again by removing the foot from the pedal. On engaging a certain lever, simultaneously depressing another pedal, and then slowly releasing it, the jeep began to move so that it could be driven around. Their parents were initially a little frightened, but soon became braver once they had recognized the harmlessness of this machine. Soon the Neanderthal fathers and mothers with their children were riding around in the jeep. The parents also quickly learned how to drive. Once when the jeep would no longer start up, they discovered the meaning of gasoline as a fuel — gasoline cans lay scattered around the crashed jet. The exact function of gasoline as a fuel was also soon determined. After examining the cylinder head, the pistons, and the spark plugs, they discovered that gasoline is burned in the cylinder head, exerts pressure on the pistons, and forces them downward. This movement was then transmitted via the crank shaft and the gears to the wheels so that the jeep finally moved due to the burned fuel.

Thus, our Neanderthal children learned about car driving and mechanics very quickly, perhaps even quicker than the Pygmy children in Central Africa who learned to drive a car within a few days, without even having seen a car or any other machine before. Thus, we are not expecting too much of our Neanderthal children.

However, the Neanderthalers were not only good botanists and naturalists, they were also thinkers. They wondered about the origin of the airplane, the machines, and the people who had died in the plane. What was the meaning of all these machines? Where did they come from? It was obvious to them that the jeep was suited to transport on the ground and the airplane to transport in the air. The hieroglyphics on the typewriter keys and the numbers on the jeep's cylinder head posed a bit of a problem. They assumed that people similar to those who had flown in the machine and thus died were certainly involved in the design and the construction of the airplane and its freight.

HOW THE NEANDERTHALERS BURY THEIR DEAD

While thinking these matters over, they were faced with a problem which needed a rapid solution: What should they do with the corpses of the air crew? Decomposition had already begun. If the crew had been Neanderthalers, they could easily have coped. They would have sent the corpses and various remains on their long journey into the other world with due and respectful preparations and a solemn religious funeral, for no Neanderthaler doubted that he was made by a Creator, and that after his death he would return to this Creator in His transcendent world. This philosophy of life and death seemed to them to be compellingly logical, for their train of thought ran like this: Just as a stone knife requires a maker, so a human body, which is more improbable than a stone knife and therefore will not develop spontaneously, also requires a creator. It was also clear to them that this Creator of the body does not live within time and space. For this reason, He lives in a transcendent world to which we all return at death. This was their clear and transparent philosophy of life and death.

The Neanderthaler also knew that after death his body would return to the clay of the earth. For this reason, he logically assumed that his body was built from the clay of the earth, as stone from the earth is converted into stone knives. Stone knives were made out of stone by the skill of a Neanderthaler—hard stones do not spontaneously organize themselves into stone knives. For this reason it seemed logical that clay was incorporated into Neanderthalers and animal bodies by a skilled hand, for clay did not spontaneously organize itself to form people and animals any more than stones spontaneously formed knives. Therefore, they reasoned that a skilled Being must have worked the clay—like the stone.

It was the Neanderthaler's life-long desire to enter into direct communication with this skilled Being. He suspected that at death this confrontation with the Clay-organizer would take place. His thoughts resulted from the simple, irrefutable observations that inorganic stones do not develop into stone knives without any external help—any more than inorganic clay could produce human, animal, and plant forms. His yearning for a meeting with his primeval Clay-organizer was increased by the persistent rumor that in the dim past some Neanderthalers had seen Him and even spoken with Him. These meetings were spoken of with great respect and fascination, although our Neanderthalers had little personal experience in this area.

Thus, the big question for the Neanderthals was this: Do these modern people, the victims of this airplane disaster, return to the same Creator as the Neanderthalers? Could they be buried in the same way as Neanderthalers? After long consultations between the wise men of the tribe, the Neanderthalers buried the modern *Homines sapientes sapientes* just as they buried their own dead. Thus, they were dispatched most honorably into the next world.

CHAPTER

2

The Neanderthalers as Rational Persons

Just as the Neanderthalers were about to bring the funeral to an end, they heard a strange noise in the jungle below their settlement. It sounded like a group of people hacking their way through the dense jungle. Occasionally shots could be heard — a novel sound to the Neanderthalers. They hesitated a little, then continued to lay the disfigured corpses, flowers, and burnt offerings in the expressly prepared coffins. The hacking noise became louder and louder, and just as the Neanderthalers were lowering the last coffin into the grave, a group of *Homines sapientes* reached the Neanderthal settlement.

LET US REASON

Both groups—Neanderthalers and *Homines sapientes sapientes*—stared in surprise, the Neanderthalers in their festive fur clothes (for the funeral) and the modern men, sweaty and tattered after their grueling journey through the jungle. After the first embarrassed salutations—for they could hardly communicate as their languages differed quite significantly—the modern men inspected the crashed airplane, for they had been sent from afar to search for the wreck.

After the modern men had discovered that all the air crew were dead and that the Neanderthalers were about to bury them respectfully, they realized that they need not fear the natives—that they were civilized. Although their dress looked different, their behavior toward the dead proved their trustworthiness.

The Neanderthalers were somewhat more solidly built, their eyebrows bushier and more prominent, and their muscles a little stronger than those of the modern men. They looked capable of throwing their spears well. Their heads too were a little larger than those of the modern men and their bodies stockier. But both their intelligence and mighty bodily strength were visible. Comparison is often difficult, but the Neanderthalers looked a little like the famous picture of Joseph, fettered in prison, discussing dreams with Pharaoh's baker and butler. The modern men (*Homines sapientes sapientes*) looked more like Pharaoh's two servants, who were conversing with Joseph.

The Neanderthalers showed great friendliness toward the new arrivals; they considered all men their friends until proven otherwise. The modern men were surprised by this friendliness, for they always acted on the customary modern principle that every man is an enemy until proven to be a friend—quite a different but widespread approach among modern, "civilized" men! Now, how were the two groups to communicate, for they shared no common language? Luckily most "primitive" men are adept at dealing with communication problems. After the Neanderthalers had left the spoil from the airplane to the modern men (they were not particularly attached to such treasures and thought that the cargo rightfully belonged to the modern men anyway), the new arrivals inquired into the purpose of the funeral ceremonies which they had observed. Why the rites, the flowers, and the offerings? Why did they respect the decaying dead?

THE NEANDERTHALERS' BELIEFS

By means of sign language, the leading Neanderthalers told the modern men that nearly all Neanderthalers believed in a transcendent but omnipresent, omnipotent Creator of man, of the world, and biology. The human body, like all animals or plants, was after all built from good clay, for once the body died it did revert to clay. Someone must therefore have shaped the clay into living human bodies, also into animals and plants, for clay could never organize itself into bodies any more than stone would spontaneously shape itself into a stone knife. The metallic airplane components—just like stone and clay—would certainly not have produced themselves to form an airplane, thus there must have been an external creator involved. Now if it is a fact that inorganic stone does not spontaneously convert itself into stone knives, and if one accepts that inorganic nonliving clay never spontaneously produces living bodies, then someone must have modeled man as he is—even modern man too—from clay. This someone must have modeled the clay just like a Neanderthaler works on stones to produce stone knives. Stones do not spontaneously turn into stone knives.

The modern men whispered and looked amused during the Neanderthaler's discourse, which displeased the polite Neanderthaler. Finally the Neanderthaler asked what the problem was, to which the modern man replied that the Neanderthaler's statement was incorrect. For salt, when it crystallizes out of water, quite spontaneously forms salt crystals. Water, when it freezes, quite spontaneously forms ice crystals. Snow falling from the sky consists of very beautiful spontaneous crystal forms. All the Neanderthalers immediately pointed out that salt crystals and snow were not alive. The modern men insisted that life is nothing but a complex crystal. Then the conversation came to a halt. Communication problems were still too extensive to permit any further useful discussion.

WHY THE NEANDERTHALERS BELIEVE

After several weeks had passed, the two groups of men began to communicate better. Less sign language was used; the Neanderthalers began to understand and also to speak the language of the *Homines sapientes sapientes*. The metaphysical unbelief of the latter very much disturbed the Neanderthalers, for together with the loss of their belief in the metaphysical, they had obviously also lost their faith in one another. The modern people showed no respect toward the dead and very little even for the living. This attitude very rapidly affected their sexual habits. For the modern men everything was free—including the attractive, intelligent Neanderthal girls. The Neanderthalers reacted very violently and sourly to the seduction of their girls by the modern men. They probably, correctly, attributed the loose morals of the modern people to their lack of respect for the metaphysical world.

One day, after both groups had begun to communicate quite well, the Neanderthal chief asked the leader of the modern men whether his unbelief toward the Creator was emotionally or rationally justified. Firmly the modern man replied that all philosophical and scientific convictions of most modern men were based on pure reason. Rationality is the key characteristic of modern man, he said, visibly taken aback by the Neanderthaler's question. But the latter continued thoughtfully and persistently to imply that the unbelief of the modern men had a purely emotional and totally irrational basis, for during their meals he had observed it to be a fact that the modern men's beliefs were based on emotions and not on rationality. Immediately the modern men took up the argument. They leaned forward to enable them to observe better around the campfire what "revelations" the Neanderthalers were about to make, for in philosophical discussions the Neanderthalers were always highly original — their thoughts were often not only original but also most ingenious.

"Yes," continued the Neanderthaler, "in the course of our mutual socializing over the past weeks, we often sat peacefully and happily at the same table with you. We prepared for you our best dishes and likewise you also shared your best food with us. So at the table our great friendship grew. Naturally we had to obtain our food fresh from the jungle. You, however, are far superior to us in some respects, for we ate from your cans and bottles. Your food, although not really fresh, tastes excellent, although we prefer truly fresh foods. Your food — sardines, ham, lentils, corn, pineapple, sausages — keeps for an unlimited time in your cans and bottles. It seems miraculous to us, for once the bottle or can has been opened, the food decays just as quickly as ours does. Furthermore, when they decay they become clay again, just as our own bodies revert to clay after death. You have told us that most modern people eat such foodstuffs which are often several years old, yet still taste quite fresh. Yes, you said that you modern people have been eating preserved food for more than one hundred years and that you have produced billions of such cans and bottles. Let us keep these facts in mind while we continue our line of argument. Is everything clear so far?"

THE NEANDERTHALERS BECOME ACQUAINTED WITH THE CONSERVED FOODS INDUSTRIES

"In our scientific discussions you have tried to convince us that our Neanderthal postulate on the need for a Creator to convert the earth's clay into our bodies and those of animals and plants is superfluous and purely emotional. You tell us modern men have proved that clay (matter) together with time periods plus energy (the warmth from the sun) suffice to ensure that clay will spontaneously organize itself into life without the aid of any creator outside of matter. For this reason, you say, the construction of a body from clay in no way proves a Creator, but only that solar energy has acted during time upon matter (clay). You have said in your language that an open physical system will and must eventually produce life, even people . . . and all this without a Creator, without metaphysics or additional intelligence, with neither plan nor teleonomy. Is that correct?"

"Yes," replied the modern men — obviously the Neanderthalers had absorbed well their lessons on evolution and biochemistry! "We are surprised that the Neanderthalers comprehend these issues so quickly and thoroughly. But what is the connection between all this and rational or emotional thoughts, and how is this connected with belief in a Creator?"

A few moments later, after some careful thought, our Neanderthaler continued to say that he could not bring the principle of bottled and canned food into agreement with the modern theories on the origin of life. The two just could not be brought to the same common denominator—sardine cans which keep almost indefinitely and the postulate of the spontaneous development of life within open physical systems.

The modern men gazed at each other with amazement, for they could not see any problems there. What was the connection? What were the Neanderthalers driving at? However, they knew the Neanderthalers well enough to expect real connections as seen by the wise Neanderthaler.

He continued, "You explained to us in our science lessons that, with time, energy plus matter (clay) spontaneously produces life, and that this life then spontaneously develops upward by mutation and natural selection, probably via a small diversion—namely us, the Neanderthalers—to form modern man. Is that so?" Somewhat ashamed by this gentle backhand, the modern men agreed. "Now," the Neanderthaler continued, "you your-selves claim to have manufactured billions of sardine cans and preserved meats. Probably you have done so constantly in large amounts over more than one hundred years." "Yes," replied the modern men, "this is indeed so, but please could we hurry up and get to the point?" Like any good Neanderthaler, however, their chief tended to think slowly, thoroughly, and very precisely.

Thoughtfully, the Neanderthaler stroked his long golden beard and said, "Did it ever occur to you in those one hundred years that the canned foods industry provides you with final proof that our postulated need for a Creator is justified and rational, and that it is the downfall of all your materialistic and atheistic theories in this area?" "No!" cried the modern men, who had congregated around the campfire to listen more closely, "We do not know what you Neanderthalers are getting at. Hurry up, we want to know." "Yes, I know that," said the wise Neanderthaler, "but first you must get back to the basics and then draw your conclusions." Naturally, the modern men were not interested in moralizing of this sort. "Well," said the Neanderthaler, "your theories state that matter (clay) plus energy plus time produces chemical evolution up to a primitive cell or a coacervate or microsphere, don't they? An open system, when it receives energy from an external source, will produce life spontaneously, with neither intelligence nor Creator to help . . . this is the irrational part of your postulate."

The modern men had long since lost patience with the Neanderthaler and wanted to finally cut him off. But he raised his hand and said quite determinedly, "Every sardine can and every glass of conserved meat must be considered as an open system so far as its energetics are concerned. The can allows heat to enter and to escape again. The can's contents can be heated or cooled at will, can it not? Therefore the system is thermodynamically completely open. Bottled meat represents an even more open system — if that is possible — for both heat and also light can easily penetrate its walls. In their energetics, both cans and glasses are widely open, thermodynamic systems. Such systems are sealed against living spores. Thermodynamically and energetically they are open. It should not matter that they are closed to living spores, for according to your theories such spores should develop easily in any place where only matter, time and energy are present. Matter and energy are plentifully available in all cans and glasses. The simple shutting out of spores in cans should not be relevant from your viewpoint. According to you, only energy, time and matter are important, and these are plentiful in each can and every glass. For this reason all sorts of simple spores should have developed long ago, for you have repeated the experiment billions of times, and this under the most favorable experimental conditions for archebiopoesis."

"In experimental reality," added the Neanderthaler, "the shutting out of spores has proved far more important than the provision of energy. According to your theories the provision of energy should be the most important factor involved in archebiopoesis in a can; but this is obviously not the case."

"How often," inquired the wise Neanderthaler, "during one hundred years of producing billions of units of canned and preserved foods, have you observed that energy in an energetically open system—such as a sardine can—plus sardine corpses (ideal material for building bodies and cells—far more so than a hypothetical primeval soup) produces new forms of—even very primitive—life? Never, by your own words. Billions of sardine experiments have shown without a doubt that energy plus matter (sardines) plus time have never produced life, not even under the most favorable conditions. This fact is so certain and so well proved that an entire industry—the canning industry—depends on it.

If this fact were not so definite and life did after all develop in these cans from time to time, then your canned foods industry would be totally useless. Why, then, do you claim the opposite to be results of this experiment, just to support your materialistic theories and postulates? We say that matter plus energy plus know-how (from a Creator or from a programmed genetic code [spore] devised by a Creator) results in life. You, however, claim that matter plus energy plus time alone gives life, and that we, therefore, require neither a Creator nor His program (spore) to conceive life. We have experimental evidence behind our faith and are therefore rational. You cannot produce a single experiment to confirm your materialistic claims!

For this reason you are, as we have already repeatedly said, purely emotional, yes, even schizophrenic—i.e., separated from experimental reality—in your beliefs. How can you aspire to being experimental scientists if you do not take the slightest notice of billions of experiments from your own industries? Experimental evidence, and therefore rationality, stand fully behind our Neanderthaler belief in a Creator. We are rational beings. You are stubborn and purely emotional and also schizophrenic in your materialism and atheism. This experiment also leaves you inexcusable, i.e. without any excuse—for your atheism and materialism."

"But let us not forget the other side of the picture. How often have you confirmed that life's spores plus matter and energy produce life (depending on the sort of spore)? Every time any of life's spores, i.e. programs, penetrate a sardine can, new life results, does it not? From this fact we Neanderthalers conclude that dead matter (clay or sardine corpses) plus energy plus life's programs produce life and that just these programs are not present in inorganic matter. Your theories require that at least occasionally in the course of billions of experiments life develop from clay (inorganic matter) and energy. Unfortunately for you and your theories this has never happened experimentally, despite billions of experiments."

The old Neanderthaler concluded his discourse with the following words: "Your unbelief in a Creator (atheism and materialism) is in no way linked to being educated in scientific experimental matters. All scientific proofs are available and all demonstrate that life only stems from life or life programs. All programs, however, finally originate from intelligent beings, without exception. Even if a computer can program itself, it initially required preprogramming by a human being to develop these programs. Now, as one or more persons are at the root of any program and as life consists of various genetic and other programs, we Neanderthalers believe in a Programmer or Creator who originally programmed us—and you, too."

"We also believe that a living Creator made us or our seed and our programs. To claim that a program programmed itself from nothing is emotional, schizophrenic, and non-rational. We Neanderthalers have learned much from you modern men—e.g. how to program certain computers. But we have also learned that only living persons devise and create programs. If we can read and decipher and program, we know that we can think in the same manner as the programmer himself. As you modern men can read the program within our own genetics, we assume that we humans can to a minor extent think as our Creator thought originally in order to program us. Thus, the programmed beings learn to understand the Programmer. We assume, therefore, that we are able to think a little as our Creator thinks. We are made in His image, therefore." The Neanderthaler closed with the impressive words: "Did not one of your thinkers say: 'We are the offspring of God!' Therefore we are the same species as God Himself, although we are fallen gods (Acts 17:28-29)." The Neanderthalers had somehow discovered one of the modern men's Bibles and had read it with much zeal!

In the following partly heated conversation, the Neanderthalers showed quite clearly their conviction that the modern men suffered more from lack of will than from lack of ability to believe. A young Neanderthaler added that the modern men did not believe because they preferred to live without belief. "Your unbelief and your atheism have no experimental/rational basis; they are purely emotion," said the Neanderthalers. "In reality they are nothing but a rebellion against your own rationale and common sense. For this reason your world is, as you have told us, filled with violent rebellion, war, murder, and destruction. You rebel against yourselves and gently need to rethink, otherwise you will destroy yourselves—and us."

Thus ended their evening together. Silently each group went its own way.

CHAPTER

3

The Neanderthalers Think Rationally

At first the modern men were very quiet and also a little stunned by the "uncivilized" Neanderthalers' arguments. But after a few days the two groups were on just as good terms again. One week later the modern men invited the Neanderthalers again to a joint meal to continue the previous conversation. All sorts of exotic dishes were presented — mostly in their conserved form, of course — for the modern men had brought all sorts of things with them.

Once the meal was over (even wine, Coca-Cola, and fruit juices had been served), the modern men's spokesman said that the

Neanderthaler's line of argument was completely wrong. It must be wrong, otherwise all modern humanity would be mistaken, for modern men today can, with no trouble, develop new life from sardine proteins in a tin can, and this without adding life spores or God's assistance! A certain scientist by the name of Sol Spiegelman had taken apart an organism (virus) and had even crystallized the dead components (the program for primitive life can be crystallized); he then put them back together again under sterile (germ-free) conditions and finally incorporated them into a new host organism. No living spore was added, but Spiegelman's virus—constructed from dead components—lived, for it underwent replication. Thus, life occurs spontaneously after all, without adding living genetic information from dead preserved matter. "If this can be done once in the laboratory, it might also have happened at the beginning of all life! So you Neanderthalers are upholding your argument with incorrect facts. The modern men's argument proves irrefutably the fact that no metaphysical God is needed to make life. Inorganic, dead chemistry is, after all, responsible for life."

At this moment the Neanderthalers appeared to be overcome by a violent fit. Even the chief Neanderthal spokesman did not seem momentarily capable of speech. Some immature modern men, having observed that this violent fit was affecting all the Neanderthalers simultaneously, decided that it must be a fit of laughter. Others attributed it to the effects of Coca-Cola on the Neanderthalers who weren't used to it. In any case, the fit soon subsided and the conversation could be continued.

The polite Neanderthaler apologized for their fit and began immediately. Their spokesman pointed out that according to the modern men's teachings it is the genetic information that produces life from the dead sardine proteins and introduces the genetic ideas into the code of the DNA molecule of its particular type (viruses, bacteria, frogs, birds, or mammals). These ideas, projects, and concepts are written on the DNA molecule in its genetic language. They are the chemical instructions required to produce life from dead proteins. "Is this not true?" The modern men agreed unanimously. "Genetics," continued the Neanderthaler, "contain the chemical instructions necessary to produce living molecules from dead ones. It could be said that genetics are a recipe book for the project of life, set in a language that we can even partly read today." The modern men confirmed the veracity of the Neanderthaler's statement.

GENETIC IDEAS

"Good," said the Neanderthaler, "then we need only take one more step to show that your modern arguments are unacceptable. Normally new life develops from the ideas which are written on zygotes in their genetic chemical language. Now your Sol Spiegelman read and understood these genetically stored ideas and transformed them into chemical reactions. Normally the genetic ideas come directly from the genetic information into the dead proteins where they organize the proteins into life. Now Sol Spiegelman injected the same genetic ideas directly into the dead chemical molecules, so that these same ideas brought the proteins to life. This proves what the Neanderthalers have always believed, that there is only one formula for life:"

matter plus energy plus ideas plus time = life

"It is all the same whether these ideas are stored in the chemistry of genetics or in Sol Spiegelman's head. The application of the ideas provides the same result—life. But without them, there is no life."

"Different ideas produce different types of life. But matter and energy without ideas give no life at all. Surely the sealed sardine cans prove this—the ideas of life (genetic projects, spores) do not penetrate into the sealed cans."

"But if ideas or concepts (*logos*) in the form of genetic information or the technical know-how of a Sol Spiegelman (again *logos/telos*) penetrate into our otherwise sealed sardine cans, they will explode with life. The ideas can even be stored in genetic language on a crystallized virus as long as a host organism is somehow present providing metabolic energy. The matter of the sardine corpses is only waiting for such concepts or ideas (*logos*, spirit, *telos*), and then it will burst into life. But without the ideas of *logos* or *telos*, not one single can of the billions produced in the entire history of the more than hundred-year-old conserved foods industry has awakened to any form of life. Provide *logos*, spirit, idea, or code—concept ('breath' or whatever) and life will spring from dead matter, just as described in Genesis. But without ideas, Spirit, breath, or *Logos*, life has never awakened in the entire history of mankind. Energy and matter never produce even a trace of life if Spirit (idea) is not added in some form."

"For this reason, we Neanderthalers believe in a *Logos*—a Creator of life—who took matter and breathed spirit, *logos*, ideas, instructions into it. Depending on the *logos*—ideas imposed on matter—the various sorts were created. But . . . no species without species-ideas! We," he said, "believe in a great, invisible Creator full of ideas or *logos*. Hence He must be a Person, for only persons have ideas which they then realize. We worship this personal Creator, who is full of ideas, as the source of all good ideas and projects. The fact that we have some ideas proves, does it not, that we were created in His image (= the same idea-filled species as God Himself). For this reason, we believe that our faith in such a Creator is fully rational, and that your belief is purely emotional. Because you only live emotionally, you live in rebellion against your own ratio and against your own rational Creator. You rebel against the experimental rational facts. For this reason, you can only believe emotionally."

"Even your Greeks knew all that, for they called this Creator '*Logos*'—the source of all ideas and projects. Life is an idea, a project, a teleonomy executed in matter. You have turned life into a non-idea, a non-project, a non-teleonomy . . . into chance. For this reason you are in a conflict with the facts of nature and are therefore without peace, rebellious, schizophrenic, and frustrated in all that you do and are."

"To claim that non-idea (= chance, stochastic molecular movements) is identical with idea, project, plan (= non-chance) is simply schizophrenic—unrelated to reality. Thus you will destroy yourselves, as well as both our world and yours."

At the end of this discussion, the young Neanderthalers discussed various possible means of solving the modern men's frustration—how it could be that *Homo sapiens* think so irrationally in the most important matters of life, i.e. in his evaluation of the meaning of life, of its origin and its destiny, despite his technical superiority to the Neanderthalers.

"They are technically advanced," said the Neanderthalers, "but philosophically and logically degenerate." This was the unanimous decision reached by the young Neanderthalers. But why were the modern men so irrational in their worldview? "Experimentally they are strong, but in the rational application of their experiments they are weak. Why?" Some considered the modern men to be the same species as the Neanderthalers, but representing somewhat degenerated Neanderthalers. Their heads, for example, were smaller. Hence it should follow that, together with the degeneration of brain volume, the skeleton and muscle strength of the modern men showed a simultaneous parallel degeneration. The capacity for logical thought was certainly degenerate, without, however, affecting his purely technical capabilities.

THE INQUISITIVE NEANDERTHALER

Small groups of Neanderthalers sat around with small groups of *Homines sapientes sapientes* and discussed further secrets of the human, animal, and plant body. The teenagers among the Neanderthalers very quickly and gladly learned the scientific secrets of the modern men. Additionally, they had time and leisure, which would not have been so easily possible under industrialized conditions. On the average, they only needed two or three hours a day to provide food and maintain their homes, then they were free.

The Neanderthalers were very impressed to discover that all the instructions and ideas required to construct a man (from clay) are present in a chemical language in every zygote from every human sperm and every human egg. They were very surprised to discover that the language of these instructions had already been partly deciphered. For example, the chemical instructions for building insulin are already known and can, when transferred into certain bacteria, be used so that the bacterium builds human insulin, although it does not require insulin for itself. As one half of all chemical instructions are from the mother and the other half from the father, the couple's children resemble their parents or their ancestors.

JOY AMONG THE NEANDERTHALERS

The Neanderthalers were most surprised to learn that on every fertilized egg (zygote) chemical instructions exist for building man and all his progeny from matter (clay). These instructions, a necessity for the construction of a man, would require an entire library containing 1,000 volumes of five hundred pages each, in the smallest print, if written in English on paper. Thus each male's sperm and each female's ovum functions like a miniaturized library filled with written chemical ideas . . . instructions to build men (or animals or plants) from clay. When the modern men showed them, on paper, how the genetic instructions looked, how they read and execute themselves (with the aid of ribosomes), how they multiply, and also correct themselves, the Neanderthalers were quite overcome with joy at the Creator's grand ideas and His incredibly miniaturized technique. They whistled and sang improvised songs about their great Creator when they discovered His wisdom in gene replication. They were literally speechless, and then again filled with wonder at the chemical miracle of cell division. The Creator's all-surpassing intelligence and His overflowing chemical and teleonomic ideas in the various instructions for building various species from clay were the topic of their evening conversation for days, of their admiration, and also of their songs.

The modern men remained totally cool and untouched at the Neanderthalers' manifestations of joy and admiration. They hardly said a word about these wonders or about their Neanderthal pupils' joy. For the modern men, the writing on the genes was no proof at all that these had either been written or developed by a Creator. For them, the laws of nature and properties of matter had written and designed everything. A Creator had nothing to do with it at all. They simply considered the Neanderthalers naive and emotional. As they attributed matter and its characteristics to purely stochastic factors, chance and the laws of nature alone were the final cause of the entire genetic code and its chemical projects. For them the entire genetic mechanism, as well as its contents, developed by chance (stochastically), for them the genetic language, with all its grammar, punctuation, correction mechanisms (necessary, should faults develop), its content of chemical ideas and projects (to build eyes, muscles, ears, livers, kidneys, hair, bones, connective tissue, hearts, lymphatics, etc.) also developed purely stochastically.

Chance was, of course, sorted out by natural selection, but natural selection itself created nothing; it only sorted out that which was supposedly provided by chance. For this reason, belief in a constructive Creator of all these organs and the information and code involved therein was considered to be totally superfluous by the modern men. The nucleotides, deoxyribose, and the guanine, thymine, uracil, cytosine, and adenine molecules supposedly formed the DNA molecule (in helical form) under the influence of the laws of nature present in all matter. At the same time—or with time—the grammar and punctuation of the genetic language developed, guided by the same laws of nature.

Chance and the laws of nature then provided plans for hearts, kidneys, brains (electronically-based computers with millions of switching mechanisms to provide intelligence and consciousness), for bones, neurons (nerves), and eyes. Also for nerve endings to equip the organism with taste and sensation, for a cerebellum to establish equilibrium, for tongues to speak, plus a computer to control the tongue and coordinate speech, for cells producing blood and lymph, hearts capable of pumping blood constantly over seventy years, while simultaneously undergoing repair processes, digestive systems, which at a slightly elevated temperature break down fats, carbohydrates, and proteins into their constituents, repair mechanisms to heal any wound—briefly, all the know-how that sets indescribably high requirements; all this developed by itself according to modern man, by chance and from the laws of nature.

THE SKEPTICAL YOUNG NEANDERTHALER

The Neanderthalers sat very still while these accomplishments of chance (stochastic phenomena) and the laws of nature were being listed. Then a young Neanderthaler, who had remained silent so far because of his youth, arose. Timidly he inquired before the older Neanderthalers and modern men whether all these accomplishments of chance and the laws of nature would fit into the categories of projects or teleonomy.

"Yes, this was certainly the case," said the modern men. "In that case," replied the young Neanderthaler, "your three laws of thermodynamics which determine all physics and chemistry must be in error, for surely the laws state that matter has neither project content nor teleonomy? So are stochastic phenomena processes that organize or disorganize? If matter is agitated, will it build a machine? Can chance plan and project a machine or devise a meaningful language, for men, animals, and plants are all biological machines built by means of a programmed language? Can chance collaborating with the non-teleonomic machine or program? If not, then your atheistic theories are nonsensical."

THE PAPER WROTE THE BOOK

The modern men remained superciliously silent. After some time the Neanderthalers' old spokesman rose again to summarize. "Really," he said, "you postulate that matter plus stochastic phenomena wrote the genetic code with its linguistic and instructional content." The modern men replied stubbornly that this was so. "Good," said the Neanderthaler, "may I then speak more clearly?" They nodded.

"In reality," he said, "you are asking us to believe that the paper on which the text of a book is written has developed not only the language in which the book is written, but also all its concepts, ideas, and thoughts. According to you, the paper wrote the entire book. Even its binding and chapter headings are due to the paper alone.

However, we, the Neanderthalers, are not prepared to believe that the paper wrote the book, including its language, ideas, vocabulary, and chapter headings, of its own accord. We regard such a postulate as schizophrenic — if I may speak so plainly," he said, "far removed from reality, i.e. schizophrenic. If the modern men believe that paper, i.e. the matter, the clay from which we are built, wrote our genetic 'recipe book' (the genetic code), then your thought processes are emotional and not rational.

We, the Neanderthalers, believe in an Author who wrote the book of life — just as any other book, without exception, was written by an author and not the paper, for life consists of various genetic books — a different genetic book for each kind of life. But as the genetic language, the genetic code, is identical in all forms of life (only the content varies, according to the sort of life), we believe in a single personal Author, who always employed the same language to store and realize all His ideas, projects, and life concepts. We regard our belief in a Creator as rational, as experimentally justifiable, far more rational than your rebellion against your own ratio (common sense), and against recognizing the Author of the genetic book of life. You must revise your thoughts immediately or you will die of emotionally-conditioned schizophrenia, totally removed from reality.[1] You are excellent technicians, but no thinkers."

The young Neanderthalers unanimously confirmed this conviction. Some of the modern men thought these arguments through; a few even revised their opinions before they broke up to return to their world. Before they left, amid many demonstrations of affection and friendship, the Neanderthalers obtained their promise not to divulge their presence in the high altitude jungles of Papua to the rest of the world. Although the Neanderthalers had come to appreciate the modern cans and machines, they preferred living primitively in a rational world of belief to spending their days in the midst of material plenty but schizophrenically in an emotional, rebellious world of unbelief.

ILYA PRIGOGINE AND ARCHEBIOPOESIS

At this stage it must be added that in 1979 Prigogine won the Nobel Prize for his work on the spontaneous structuring of systems in a state of non-equilibrium.[2] This was used throughout the world by materialists (and also by Prigogine) to prove the possibility of spontaneous biogenesis from unstructured matter. In this manner the impossibility, according to the second law of thermodynamics, of spontaneous structuring upward to finally result in life was thought to have been avoided.

This somewhat premature conclusion regarding the possibility of a spontaneous structuring of matter into life (biogenesis) reached by the materialists must be considered, keeping in mind that Prigogine only investigated systems well out of equilibrium. Such systems are, therefore, irreversible and have nothing in common with the organic-chemical systems of reactions which might possibly be involved in biogenesis. Such organic-chemical systems, which supposedly spontaneously provided the original building materials of life, are, of course, as every organic chemist knows, strictly reversible (apart from certain known "entropy holes"), so that Prigogine's otherwise so important work is totally irrelevant here.

CHAPTER

4

Creation or Chance?

Thought processes should lead to every conviction, i.e. to every belief—or also to every unbelief—unless emotions overshadow or eliminate those thought processes. The convinced atheist—believing that there is no God—as well as the theist, who by means of deliberations and thought processes has come to the conclusion that a Creator does exist—each should reach his conviction by thought processes rather than by mere emotional sway.

It is impossible to force oneself to a belief in anything. If we try to force ourselves into any belief without thought processes, the result is a hysteria, which differs vastly from a true conviction or a genuine belief. If any sect were to require of its followers the "belief" that Jonah swallowed the whale, then they could certainly force themselves to do so purely emotionally, in order to believe such a dogma. However, the belief in this dogma would be purely emotionally based hysteria and would have little connection with any really rational conviction. Thus many people try to believe emotionally in the dogmas of a religion which are, however, often as nonsensical and irrational as the dogma that "Jonah swallowed the whale." It is just for this reason that many churches and congregations suffer from dangerous emotionalism and hysteria. Ratio — i.e., a good reason for rationally accepting a dogma — would lead to genuine conviction and thus also to a powerful faith, for man is rightly called *Homo sapiens* — he is not satisfied until convinced rationally. Only after a man is convinced and acts accordingly is he justifiably flooded by emotions such as love, joy, and peace — after satisfying his ratio. If however, he does not obey and use his ratio, he is overcome by negative emotions — hysteria, frustration, disappointment, and unhappiness.

Thus, belief is a sort of rational conviction — a certain faith in rational, even though often invisible, hopes. However, it cannot be forced without thought processes. A rational basis for the conviction must exist — even if the basis of this conviction is the existence of an omnipotent, omniscient God.

THE FOUR PILLARS OF FAITH

Now which kind of conviction (belief, faith) regarding the existence of an almighty God can we hold rationally? Four different beliefs exist.

1. There is no Creator God. Matter was and is eternal and therefore requires no Creator to make it and the life springing from it. This belief is called atheism.

2. There is an almighty Creator who may be personal or not, who created and maintains the world. This belief is called theism.

3. There is an almighty Creator who in the beginning created the world and biology. He may be personal or not. But since the time He created and "wound up" everything, He no longer involves Himself with His creation anymore; He simply allows it all to "run down." This belief is called deism and is often linked with the "God is dead" theology.

4. An almighty Creator exists who is, however, identical with the cosmos and the matter of the universe. All men and all molecules of the universe are a part of this omnipresent Creator. The Hindus believe this. For this reason they think that they and all animals are parts and various aspects of God. This conviction is called pantheism. The God of the pantheists is usually taken impersonally.

In the previous chapters we have seen that it is difficult to defend the atheistic solution of the God-dilemma truly rationally. The evidence of the properties of matter demonstrates it is not creative. So how can creation be explained without a Creator if matter itself is not creative?

In considering this question it must be remembered that the properties of matter and energy must have been constant from the beginning; otherwise primitive carbon would not have been carbon in the modern sense of the word. Now if matter and energy today are not creative, then accordingly they were not creative in the beginning either, for their properties have by definition remained constant. Under these conditions we must ask ourselves why in the beginning life supposedly developed from matter and energy spontaneously, but today it does not. The only squarely rational reply to this question is, of course, that at biogenesis an environment different from that known to us today acted on primitive nature. But in principle, from the point of our time-space continuum, our material and environment has remained the same. Why did "spontaneous" biogenesis take place then and not today?

We are compelled to suggest a different type of environment, an environment of ideas which in those days acted upon the matter (which in itself was "idea-less") and which no longer acts in nature today; for matter, then as now, is itself without ideas. For this reason it needs—now as it did then—to be acted upon by ideas in order to bring about biogenesis. Now we are on the right track, for the ideas of a biochemist do bring matter to life today—as they did in the beginning. Experimental evidence from the laboratory proves this fact over and over again. Providing matter with a rational environment, i.e. one of *logos* or *telos*, produces life today—as it did in the beginning. Only thus can the fact be explained that matter with constant non-creative properties does and did carry, again and again, the concepts of life.

Logos-mind acts on matter and energy now as it did then to produce the ideas and concepts of life. At this stage of insight it is simply no longer possible to remain either an atheist or a materialist. The facts simply preclude both of these philosophies. So at this stage we will not enter into belief Number 1 (atheism) any further. But how are we to cope with the three other possibilities: theism, deism, and pantheism? How are we to form an opinion here?

Both deism and theism can presuppose a personal or an impersonal God. Pantheism normally requires an impersonal God, for there God is nature and nature is God. If the term "nature" is taken only to include matter and energy, then obviously this God cannot be personal, for the universe of inorganic matter is obviously not "personal" in the usual sense of the word. Raw matter is neither intelligent nor does it possess consciousness, as far as we know; therefore it is impersonal.[1]

Once we have established that a Creator must exist, we must pose our second question: Is the Creator personal or not? Of course, we cannot imagine or conceive an omnipresent, eternal, or omnipotent Being—whether personal or not—for our thought apparatus is not capable of imagining anything unlimited or infinite. We can, for example, only think aided by temporal limitations, one thought after the next, which we express by the term "time." If we speak of the term "eternity," our thought apparatus can no longer cope, for "eternity" thoroughly eliminates time—and thus a component of our thoughts.

Thus with even our best will we are incapable of sensibly contemplating the term "eternity" or an eternal God, for our sense (thought) is limited by time. For this reason, we do not wish to be so unreasonable as to attempt thoughts about an eternal, omnipotent God. We must abstain from attempts to enter into

51

unlimited, eternal thoughts, for in this area we will produce no sense. It is just for this reason that so many religions attempting to deal with God, the eternal, contradict each other and make little sense. They must be contradictory, for "God, the Eternal, the Almighty, the Unlimited" cannot be successfully dealt with by our thought apparatus. So we shall avoid thoughts and questions of this sort which only prove indigestible to our minds.

PERSONAL OR IMPERSONAL?

The question of whether or not God is personal is more easily approached by our thought apparatus. Also the question of His intelligence can be investigated by us. Intelligence is often defined as the capacity to profit from past experience. Thus, intelligence requires a memory—so that the past can be taken into account. However, an eternal God cannot possess a memory in our sense of the word, because for Him there are no events in the past to consider. Everything is in the eternal present! But within our time-space continuum He can have profit from a memory, otherwise He would be less than His creation, less than we are, if He possessed no memory in our dimension. As the greater creates the lesser, God must be greater than man and therefore possess—seen from within time—a longer memory and greater intelligence than man.

But is something intelligent always and automatically a person? No, for a properly programmed computer can learn to play chess better than I can and thus it will eventually beat me. So, according to our definition this machine is certainly intelligent. But is it therefore automatically a person? No, for the intelligent computer has no consciousness, i.e. no self-recognition (*Cogito, ergo sum*). Higher animals can reflect on themselves to a small degree. Certain types of apes recognize themselves in the mirror and probably reflect on themselves. Even less intelligent animals such as cows practice a pecking order—one cow is the leader and allows no other cow to go first—and hence reflects on its position in the herd.

We practice self-reflection and are therefore persons. However, our personality has very little to do with our intelligence. Certain people, who are without doubt personalities, do not need to be very intelligent. Here again, we shall apply the same principles of thought to decide whether God is a person in this sense of the word: the greater made the lesser. If we are persons with self-reflection then accordingly God must be a greater Person with greater self-reflection. By this principle He can hardly be less than a person—even a sub-person—He can hardly be less than the people He created. For this reason we assume that God must be super-Person. This leads to the thought that He not only reflects on Himself; He will also reflect on us—our deeds and our behavior. People reflect on other people. He will also adapt His mode of action according to our deeds: intelligence requires that He should profit from our mode of action, as He possesses a memory for us within time.

If God is a super-intelligent, super-personality (for His creatures, people, are after all intelligent personalities and for this reason the Creator must surpass them in intelligence and personality), He will also be capable of expression—He will "speak," express His ideas and even put them into practice. Briefly, He must be a great *Logos* (Word)—just as man is a lesser *logos*. Thus our rational thought processes would lead us to the statement that God must be a personal *Logos*, for if He is only an intelligent spirit who neither speaks nor expresses Himself, then He would be less than a person, and He would be impersonal or less than personal.

These thoughts result from the principle that the superior created the inferior. Man could perhaps synthesize a virus or a bacterium, for viruses and bacteria are incomparably less complex than man. But our Creator, who must be infinitely intelligent and a super-personality to us, could never be created by us, for as a super-personality He is far greater than men who are mere personalities. The Bible, of course, teaches that the Creator is super-intelligent. Additionally, He possesses a super-consciousness, for He reflects on His super-self (the three Persons of the Trinity love each other—the Father loves the Son and has given everything into His hands [John 3:35]). Also He is the *Logos* and has developed ideas and projects which He expresses. As *Logos* He wrote the Ten Commandments "with His own hand," as reported by Moses.

PHILOSOPHIZING AND ITS LIMITATIONS

In this area, however, little progress is made by philosophizing. For this reason we shall leave this aspect of faith as it is. Let us now approach another very urgent question. Can man as man sensibly experience such a super-Being if such a super-personality really does exist? Surely an important pleasure in life is meeting with other personalities, experiencing them, and gaining from this experience. Surely we are all enriched most by meeting and experiencing again and again true personalities during our careers. I personally owe very many treasures of all sorts to contacts with other personalities.

Now if a super-intelligent, super-Person who is my Creator does exist, and if I was created in His image (although much smaller, yet in His image in thought-structure), then I will profit and be enriched by any contact with Him. Also if He created us in His image and I resemble Him and He is like me as a person to a certain extent, then He will desire fellowship with others like us, for people are interested in one another—if they are normal people—otherwise they are sick.

Our next question must be: Can I establish contact with the super-personality that is my Creator? Surely it is clear that I as a limited human being cannot comprehend Him, as He is unlimited, eternal, almighty, omniscient, and omnipotent, which must be strictly incomprehensible to me. So any contact on a sensible basis is simply impossible. Thus, there remains only one possibility for establishing sensible contact—the super-Creator would have to come down to our wavelength. He would have to become a man such as we are. The only way for an animal to really understand a man is for it to become a man. If I had been born as a calf, I would have no difficulty in understanding cow language.

If a man wishes to understand God's language there are only two means of overcoming the speech barrier between God and man: (1) man becomes God, or (2) God becomes man. Only if (1) or (2) occur will God and man be on a common wavelength, and only then will they really be able to communicate.

CONTACT BETWEEN PERSONALITIES

We must still ask ourselves another basic question: How is contact with another person established in the first place? How does one "experience" another person? It is very important to find the correct reply to this question, otherwise misunderstandings will arise later on.

Who and what the personality of a human (or an animal) is, no one really knows. It is not simply the thought capacity of a man, for a computer thinks (thus it possesses thought capacity)—and even thinks much more rapidly than man—yet the computer is no personality. A personality reads the perceptions of its computer-brain but is not only a computer (brain) or thought capacity. A TV faithfully reproduces pictures of the distant reality without ever being aware of the image on its screen. It is the person outside the TV sitting in front of the screen who is aware of the picture. Neither the brain nor the TV perceive; this is done by the ego, the personality. It is the personality which lives outside the dimension of the electronic machine (the brain, the wiring) that is aware; just like the person sitting in front of the TV is experiencing perception while living in a different mechanical dimension from that of the TV itself. Man possesses an additional dimension to the TV—that of his personality, which perceives. The TV itself does not perceive, although it projects the image onto the screen.

Thus man's personality lives in a dimension of its own, in a world of perception. It does not live in the world of machines, which have no personality and therefore cannot perceive.

This fact has an important consequence: it is only possible to contact a personality indirectly via its TV apparatus, i.e. via its five senses, through the wiring of the brain. The person himself is separated from the purely material world by an event horizon. The material world is presented to the person under the guise of electronic pictures of reality. The person himself is hidden, and materialistic science has not yet discovered the secret of personality and will not discover it either, for materialistic science does not believe in other dimensions, realities which are in principle inaccessible from time and matter.[2] And it is in such a dimension, concealed from our present-day research, that human personality in God's image exists within its own dimensions.

CONTACT WITH THE CREATOR?

Here we are brought back to our central question: How will the Creator meet us and we Him? How is a dialogue established with Him? How does He approach us? First we must realize that a dialogue requires two personalities—the speaker and the listener. Both must speak and both must also listen. The major question concerning the Creator and us is and remains quite practical: How?

It is impossible to argue over or discuss certain things. As C.S. Lewis once said, it is impossible to philosophize (at least with any prospect of success) whether or not the cat is in the linen cupboard. The cat can neither be seen nor heard. It is just absent. There is only one means of discovering whether the cat is in the cupboard, i.e. go to the cupboard, open the door, and look in—and there she is, purring happily.

Similarly, there is only one method of experiencing a personality, for it (the personality) is, so to speak, sitting behind its event horizon in the cupboard in its other dimension. We miss it and seek it. No amount of philosophy will help here; one must go and search for it where it is—in the dimension of personality.

In a great crowd thousands of people are to be seen. It is possible to select one person or also a small group from the crowd and to attempt a dialogue with him. If a reply is forthcoming, the mutual experience has begun. If there is no reply, I can do nothing to bring about a dialogue. We are here, of course, referring to experiencing a personality by means of a dialogue. Now, is such an experience objective or subjective? This is an important point! For the experience of another person is, essentially, purely subjective and not objective. Thus, another personality is experienced via one's own personality, i.e. purely subjectively. It is therefore in the nature of a personal encounter, of a personal experience or of a dialogue with another personality, that it is subjective and not objective. Thus also is our experience of the super-personality which we call the Creator. This experience and this encounter with Him must, by its nature, be purely personal, subjective, and confined to the individual heart, soul, or personality. It is impossible to philosophize or argue about it objectively. Perhaps it may be possible to see objectively that a person has met and experienced a great personality, for such an encounter would not leave him unchanged. How much more would it be impossible for a subjective encounter with the super-personality called our Creator to leave us unaffected!

Innumerable witnesses are alive today who obviously have come out of such an encounter as totally changed people. The Bible speaks of many such changed people and refers to such a powerful experience as being born again.

These facts cannot be denied simply because they are subjective or because such a rebirth has not been experienced personally. Of course, all such encounters are subjective, and not everyone does experience such an encounter. The very nature of such an encounter with another personality requires it to be subjective. Therefore, it must always remain the subjective secret of those who have made the encounter — although they can witness such an encounter. Why is it then that very many people seek such an encounter with their Creator—and do not find it?

The reason is very simple if we ask ourselves a further simple question: What hinders most the mutual subjective experience of two personalities? How is it that husband and wife can totally miss experiencing or really encountering one another in the same house? Although they live together, their souls are lonely. Why do they not experience each other's personalities? Because the one personality has often made itself impossible with the other. If I am insulted, lied to, abused, or even ignored and left to myself by another person, I will, of course, consider this behavior impossible.

The opposite, of course, applies too! People behaving thus will never find each other and their respective personalities. People who unjustifiably write or speak evil of me (and if I become aware of this), will not experience me unless they fulfill one condition—that the culprit, if he really values my acquaintance, comes to me to apologize. I must, of course, act likewise if I am at fault, otherwise I shall never personally experience and enjoy my partner either.

The theologians of the past understood this fact much better than many of their colleagues do today, for in the past they taught that fellowship between two persons was harmed by infringing the laws governing personal relationships. Speaking plainly, sin between two persons (to use the old theological term) separates them. Until the infringement is removed between the people and they are thus reconciled, fellowship between the two will not be reestablished.

These facts demonstrate that in the past the nature of our personality and the laws governing personal relationships were perhaps better understood than today, for today some think that by a forced dialogue between two estranged people, fellowship and mutual experience are possible, even without complete reconciliation. Only a thorough reconciliation brings two estranged persons together again. But without this, no true interpersonal fellowship or experience can be reestablished. As none of us are perfect, this thorough reconciliation has to happen again and again if interpersonal fellowship and real encounters are to be permanent and also to grow.

Could this not provide at least one explanation for the fact that many people never in their lifetime experience the super-personality of their Creator? They are not reconciled with their Creator. Have you perhaps ignored your Creator up to now, have you never thought about Him? Never taken the time to speak to Him in your heart? Have we never seriously sought Him in reconciliation? One can hardly experience a person by simply ignoring him, not even if this person is our Creator. Or could it be that we have even denied or hated Him, although He has obviously done so much for us? Or have we despised or denied His good commandments? Thou shalt not steal. Thou shalt not commit adultery. Thou shalt not bear false witness. Or let us consider the summary of all God's commandments: "Whatsoever ye would that men should do to you, do ye even so to them: for this is the law and the prophets" (Matthew 7:12).

Today, we hardly can deny that this summary of the law would solve all political, economical, and also most social problems of our poor world. Yet because we want to be free today from

God's infamous Ten Commandments, the socialists of the world burden and molest us with innumerable other little parliamentary laws—simply because they want to rid themselves in practice of God's simple Ten Commandments.

If now God's Ten Commandments have been disobeyed by us personally, although God entrusted them to us with the best intentions, we will never be able to experience God's personality, for we have thus made ourselves unacceptable to Him. We have ignored or despised His good commandments and are therefore not reconciled to Him, for love of God or of anyone else always includes an initial resolution of enmity, of alienation through reconciliation.

Here we have the basis of all genuine fellowship with the Creator's personality—and with all other personalities. We know God's commandments which serve to govern our relationship to Him and to our fellowmen. And no doubt we have ignored or disobeyed them. For this reason we have become unacceptable and therefore estranged to each other.

How can we find the necessary reconciliation? By asking for forgiveness, if we are serious about this encounter, and this is certainly quite right. If, however, we have done something that needs to be forgiven, who will pay the price of this debt? The price (the fine) for our sin is high. The Bible teaches that the wages of sin (the price for breaking His good laws governing fellowship) is death, i.e. elimination of all mutual fellowship, which equals death.

CHAPTER

5

He Who Thinks
Has to Believe

Over the centuries, many leading thinkers were also religious. They were, of course, not all Christians, but to a large extent they believed in God, i.e. they were theists. People like Voltaire, Marx, and Lenin, who provide the exception to this rule, have always existed. But the exception proves the rule. Thinkers such as Isaac Newton, Blaise Pascal, and Michael Faraday certainly represent the majority of the thinkers. The great thinker Paul is an eminent example of this conviction. Such men found confirmation of their belief in God—and in some cases of their Christianity—through their rational thought and experience.

Many thinkers of today hold the opinion that Albert Einstein was the greatest scientist of all time. His mathematical, logical thoughts on the origin and nature of the universe led him too to a firm, logical belief in the Creator. Above all, his scientific knowledge motivated him to seek to comprehend the method of creation used by the mysterious (to him) but rational Creator—Einstein came to the conclusion that God did not create by chance, but rather that He worked according to planned, mathematical, teleonomic, and therefore (to him) rational guidelines. For Einstein and others, chance was an antipode, an antithesis to thought, which he therefore completely excluded as a means of creation by a thinking Creator.

He attributed creative, logical thoughts, plans (= teleonomy) to God and thus decisively rejected the modern fashion of attributing all that exists to chance and therefore to non-thought, non-teleonomy, and non-logic. The presumption that a thinking, intelligent Creator employed non-thought, i.e. chance, to create was therefore quite unacceptable to Einstein; for to accuse any intelligent person of non-thought in his work would upset and insult him enormously.

It is, of course, clear that Einstein did not claim to be a Christian. His convictions in metaphysical matters reached only to a firm belief in a Creator, which motivated Einstein's research in mathematics and physics. Einstein desired to grasp the creative methods employed by God to make the world, for to him the greatest miracle in the universe was that we can at least in part comprehend it. We can have our own sensible, logical thoughts about creation. So these conform to the laws of human sense and thought. From this Einstein concluded that the universe (and therefore biology) must have its origin in understanding, thought, concept, mathematics, intelligence, and teleonomy, and not in randomness—chance plus the inanimate laws of nature.

We can say with Einstein that our sense and our thought processes must have something in common with that creative sense and with that creative logic that made the world, for we are capable of at least partly comprehending and following His creative thoughts, even if this capacity is restricted. We are, in principle, capable of thinking on the creative wavelength—even if our thoughts will never quite comprehend His thoughts. We slowly begin to have presentiments from afar of the same formative and the same mathematical thought processes as those used by the Creator.

Einstein is, of course, not the only person who has to be mentioned here. Sir James Jeans, the great physicist, Max Planck, the author of the quantum theory, and Sir James Simpson, who discovered the soporific effect of chloroform in surgery . . . these were all great thinkers and scientists whose thoughts were influenced by an active belief in the Creator. Simpson was even a diligent evangelical Christian and evangelist.

Now, why is it that these men, like many other scientists, were completely convinced believers in God whereas other thinkers such as Voltaire, Marx, or Lenin came to the opposite conviction regarding a Creator? For some thinkers, then, thoughts and science confirmed their theistic beliefs, while for the others the opposite was the case. Is then thought itself worth so little?

Today we still find exactly the same paradox among thinking people. For some people their thoughts seem to confirm their theistic belief whereas others are led in the opposite direction by their thought processes. Does thought then lead astray? Is it in itself unreliable? If thought is an unreliable means of reaching a logical goal, then thought and philosophy should be given up completely! But then we should cease to be *Homo sapiens*, for we would thereby give up our very species—the species that thinks! In this case it would be better to live as an apathetic non-thinker, interested only in sensual pleasures such as eating and drinking, than to be an incorrect thinker, enthusing in thought processes which will only lead to the wrong goal anyway.

Why can thinkers such as Horkheimer, Habermas, or Marcuse of the School of Frankfurt become decided atheists through their thoughts, while a physicist like Walter Heitler becomes a committed Christian through his thoughts? How is it that eminent scientists such as F.H.C. Crick[1] claim that biology is better understood by physics and chemistry than through the supernatural and metaphysics? Crick is convinced that the scientific thinker would sooner believe in chemistry and physics as the science of life than in metaphysics. Why the "either chemistry or metaphysics" explanation of the origin and meaning of biology? Are these explanations contradictory, or do they supplement each other? Do they really exclude each other as Crick and countless others seemingly assume?

Very many scientists today think just like Crick. They assume that the existence of an understood chemical or physical basis of life—of a known chemical cell metabolism—automatically excludes a metaphysical basis of life: "As soon as we understand cell chemistry, we know that a metaphysical explanation of life becomes superfluous." As this school of thought is taught avidly and dogmatically, indeed almost universally, in most schools and high schools, we must consider it more closely, for many honest thinking scientists are absolutely and unshakeably convinced that the mere existence of proof for a chemical basis of life and of cell metabolism automatically and simultaneously totally excludes any metaphysical basis of life.

Thus, a thinker who knows the Krebs cycle or the Embden-Meyerhof pathway and realizes their significance in providing biology with energy will, according to the above principle of thought, automatically put in question any metaphysical basis of life. According to the modern school of thought, this is the enlightened approach which is far superior to and more intelligent than the ideas of those thinking in metaphysical terms, who still believe in God as a real biological factor. At least many scientists, including myself, were brought up in this manner in our biochemistry laboratory.

A physical-chemical explanation of the basis of life thus supposedly destroys all metaphysical superstition within the realm of biology—this is the modern parole. Supposedly "science destroys religion." Is this so?

Crick and many others like him thought that the mere discovery of the fact that man and all biological beings are, materially seen, chemically based machines and mechanisms, simultaneously, authoritatively, and automatically discredited metaphysics as the basis of the origin and nature of man and biology. The assumption is quietly made, of course, that the time-space continuum represents the entire universal reality.

It is for this reason, that, from a scientific viewpoint, no metaphysical reality can exist. If it does not exist then of course it simply cannot have provided the biological mechanisms for man or for biology. Therefore, once man's chemical and physical basis and the mechanisms involved have been discovered, there is nothing more left to discover about man.

So how did Crick reach the conviction that every newly understood metabolic pathway progressively excludes a metaphysical origin of life? This opinion rules almost the entire thinking scientific world today, although it is obviously irrational.

In order to prevent any misunderstanding, we shall repeat Crick's belief once more: each newly understood chemical metabolic pathway renders any metaphysical origin of life even more unlikely than it was before this discovery.

What exactly does this conviction express? In reality, just that every new piece of understanding concerning the mode of action of any machine will render more unlikely the creation and conception of this machine by an engineer outside the machine! Thus, the greater our understanding of any machine mechanisms, the less likely it becomes that the machine was designed and built by an engineer outside the machine! The more we understand how the machine functions, the more certain it becomes that no engineer, but the machine itself (made of matter), built the machine! In other words, the better we understand the mechanism and functions of a cylinder head, the more certain it becomes that the iron of the cylinder head (or light metal) designed and constructed the head! The better we understand a radio, the more certain does it become that the wires built the apparatus itself!

Crick's statement is obviously slightly irrational! Those scientists who believe similarly must also be irrational! Perhaps the Neanderthalers were right after all in their evaluation of modern man—that he is emotional and not rational. In reality, of course, says Crick, the greater the complexity of the machine and its functions, the more certain it is that non-teleonomic matter built them without design from outside! This constitutes modern logical ability?!

OUR DOG

When we were still children on the farm in England, we had a faithful guard, a sheepdog, who loved us children very much. Nothing could ever have happened to us in the dog's presence, for she always looked after us and our parents faithfully. One day when my father was suddenly attacked in the open field by a furious Wessex saddleback sow whose young had temporarily been taken away for veterinary reasons, the dog, at great risk to her own safety, of course, reacted immediately and bit firmly into the raging animal's hock and held on with all her strength until my father and we children could run to safety. I have never forgotten that—the great loyalty, intelligence, and immediate understanding of our sheepdog, Folly. The same sort of thing sometimes happened to us with the geese who often became angry, especially when with their young ones, and then attacked us. The dog always defended us adroitly.

Folly was a female, and once when she had her own pups, we unwittingly went into her kennel and took the newly born puppies into our hands. Normally a new mother would have bitten us immediately, for no one is ever allowed to touch the puppies. But she only begged us with her eyes and with whimpers to give her the puppies back. I can still see her glowing eyes today. My parents were very angry with us when they discovered what we had done in our ignorance.

Now, our dog Folly had one great weakness; she loved to lie on Mother's couch in the living room. But at certain times of the year she always shed her coat, which was not exactly good for the lovely couch. So she was banned from the couch, which she understood very well. She then avoided the couch, at least she did so in Mother's presence. One evening the entire family was out. Folly was locked into the kitchen so that she could not be tempted to misuse Mother's couch. Yet there was one way by which she could still procure a pleasant evening on the couch: Folly knew how to open certain doors. A small back staircase connected the kitchen with the hall and the living room via a large main oak staircase. Obviously, the following happened: hardly had we left when Folly opened a kitchen door, trotted up the back staircase, then down the large front main staircase and then walked through the living room over to the couch, where she made herself wonderfully comfortable.

Now when we came home in the Bentley late that evening, our dog heard us from afar—the exhaust on those cars could hardly be missed! Obviously, she must quickly have trotted up the front staircase and down the back stairs into the kitchen, where she was waiting to greet us, as usual. Normally she was overjoyed at our arrival. But this time she was clearly miserable; she tried to grin (she could do that very well indeed), but without success. Her tail was between her legs and she slunk around us all—she wanted to rejoice, for she loved us, but she simply could not.

My father noticed this immediately and asked her what she had done now — one could talk to the dog very well. With every word Folly's misery visibly increased and now she even began to whimper. Mother understood quicker than Father. She had stolen nothing. So she took Folly straight to the couch, which of course was covered with hair. My mother scolded her properly and gave her a few hard slaps. Folly then lay down on her back, thus of course exposing all the soft parts of her abdomen. In this manner dogs demonstrate their capitulation. From then on the opponent can do whatever he likes with the one who capitulates thus. The victor, if he is a dog, could of course immediately tear out a dog's bowels in this position. Thus this position demonstrates total capitulation.

My father, who understood dogs well, then gave the dog some signs of affection and forgiveness (stroking her and talking to her kindly). She stood up, licked his hands and those of my mother (hands that had punished her) and went humbly but confidently to her food in the kitchen. Fellowship with the family had been reestablished by capitulation, followed by reconciliation.

RECONCILIATION AND FELLOWSHIP

If a Creator does exist (a fact which any non-prejudiced, thinking person must surely admit), who is super-intelligent, omniscient, omnipresent, and super-personal, it is only to be expected that He would be interested in His creation in the form of people. As both — Creator and created — are persons, both sides will be capable of cultivating personal fellowship. However, they will only find such fellowship within the laws governing interpersonal behavior. If sin (infringement of these laws) of any sort exists between the two parties, it will have to be removed by capitulation and reconciliation before fellowship can be really enjoyed.

The above principles provide us with a reply to the problem of a subjective experience of God's personality, which some experience and others do not. Everyone can experience His personality on the basis of capitulation and reconciliation, for Christ became man and died to make this reconciliation available to all people. Naturally, only those people who recognize their need to be reconciled will experience this reconciliation, for it was not necessary to die for the self-righteous to reconcile them!

Christ's forgiveness reestablishes the interpersonal contact between God and man through reconciliation. But it is only with personal reconciliation and forgiveness that one begins to establish fellowship with God and to enjoy Him. Only then does one begin to enjoy His beauty, character, and perfection. It is, perhaps, justified to say that all tensions and estrangements in Christian and other circles develop because people do not know this joy or because they no longer actively cultivate it. Even in God's material creation we can feel something of this overflowing creative joy. The sheer beauty of the tulip, of Daphnia in March, of lilac in May, and of asters in autumn all testify to this joy. The leaping calves and laughing young people that we see everywhere testify of the same great joy of the Creator. Even the shadows of death yield to the glory of the resurrection.

But how can mortal men experience fellowship with such an eternal, joyous, resurrecting Creator? The difference between

Him and us is too great; we cannot establish direct fellowship with Him. Our wavelength is too different from His wavelength. God lives in a dimension which is sealed off from our dimension of time and matter by an event horizon. The species difference between God and humans is so great that it cannot be bridged directly. In addition, we are, as sinners, unacceptable to God, which would exclude real fellowship even if we could approach Him.

THE GOD-MAN

When Christ became man He revealed God's nature and character in human form. This is a tremendous fact; God, the eternal Creator, from now on is "on the same wave-length" as humans. God became a real biological man of the same biological species just like we are. To this is added another and even greater fact: since Christ never gave up His adopted humanity, a true Man has remained God. "Whosoever has seen Me [the Man] has seen the Father [God]," said Jesus Christ (John 14:9). "I and the Father are one" (John 10:30). These words show that Christ is the second Person of the Trinity and that He was God before He became man and remained God even as a man.

Now we are in a position to understand a little better God's person, His ways with us, His thoughts and His plans, for since the resurrection of Christ, a Man, Christ, the God-man is ruling God's throne. The rule of the heavenly kingdom lies in the hands of a Man who loves men so much that He died for them and rose again from the dead. The Man to whom was given all power in heaven and on earth speaks as we do, thinks as we do, rejoices as we do, knows the troubles of life and death as we do, for He died as we do, and rose from the dead as we all shall. At last, complete communication, complete fellowship between man and God and God and man is possible. Two types of personalities—man and God-man—are indeed reconciled.

Thus God's plan for us becomes plain. He wants to make renewed beings out of us so that we cannot only regain our original purpose at creation but so that we even surpass it. It will be far more glorious with us than with Adam in paradise. Christ's character led to His crucifixion—but with the crucifixion it led also to the greatest conceivable glorification of God. Thus was an entire world saved to a new kind of life, for men will make Christ's attitude their goal, resulting in an almost equally great glory. God's image, but even better than in the beginning in Adam's paradise, is God's purpose for us. For this reason we also have to go through the shadow of death here on earth just like Christ did. But we must never lose the goal from our sight, for in both cases the goal is paradise with God Himself, who created us for this eternal purpose.

MAN AS GOD

Any scientifically-thinking person will immediately ask whether God really did historically become man in Christ— whether the entire story was not an invention of the disciples later on. We can best resolve these doubts by asking ourselves what we would expect of a man who in his inner self was and is God the Creator. If we formulate such a question, we find that the entire biblical report on Christ appears to be genuine on all counts, and also that it is uniform. Seldom does a forged report agree in all details like the report on Christ. Just try to present some thought-up story to any experienced judge! The judge will nearly always discover contradictions if the story really is a fake. But Christ's entire historical testimony fits together perfectly. The internal uniformity of the report does ring true. Let us examine the following reports for their veracity:

Before Christ died, He clearly told His disciples and the world that He was going to Jerusalem to die there for the propitiation of all men's sins. However, He added clearly that after three days He would rise again from the dead. What normal mortal man would dare to make two such predictions?

The Pharisees reported this prediction that He would rise after three days to Pilate, for the words of Christ were well-known everywhere. What would happen to the Pharisees if these prophecies really were fulfilled? For this reason, the Pharisees requested guards for the grave to prevent any theft of the corpse (Matt. 27:6). The officer on crucifixion duty and who saw Christ die spontaneously testified that the Man who was crucified was truly the Son of God (Matt. 27:54). Over five hundred people saw Christ after His crucifixion and His death (1 Cor. 15:6). Some of them talked with Him about biblical and other subjects, and even ate with Him. These people could easily have contradicted the apostle Paul's report, for at that time many of them were still living. No normal person who had thus been crucified and martyred could have recovered as well after three days as Christ did.

Lazarus' resurrection four days after his public burial took place quite openly. Even Christ's enemies, the Pharisees, could not deny the truth of this resurrection testimony; it was much too well-known. This even provided an excellent testimony that

Christ was the Son of God, which the Pharisees simply could not deny. For this reason, they tried to undo Christ's deed by plotting to kill Lazarus, for many people believed on the Son of God as a logical consequence of Lazarus' resurrection.

The feeding of the five thousand and of the four thousand continued in another way the same testimony to Christ's deity. Either these testimonies are true, or they are not true. The evidence for their truth is, however, so strong that even the Pharisees were prepared to take to murder to erase it. It was so strong that there was such a great gathering of the people coming and going continually so that Christ did not even have time to eat (Mark 6:31).

Could any different behavior from that of Christ be expected if God really became man? If God truly became man, then surely we would expect Him to become a man like Christ became. Would we expect Him to become an abnormal man like many of our present kings, ministers, presidents, or dictators? If God as man had appeared in pomp, then many people would quite rightly doubt whether God really did become a real man. The life story of Christ in the Gospels and also in Isaiah corresponds with what we would expect of a human being who really is God the Highest. One only has to read carefully through the gospel of John to become convinced by the evidence of the Lord Jesus Christ's superiority in character. The internal evidence for the truth of John's testimony shines clearly through every sentence of this unique account.

A FEW CONCLUSIONS

Two types of evidence or report exist which give us information about the Creator's nature: (1) The evidence provided by creation itself, which is well-known to all thinking, observant people, irrespective of whether or not they possess the Holy Scriptures. Our Neanderthalers have shown us what conclusions honest, thinking people can reach, even though they do not own a Bible. (2) The evidence provided by the Holy Scriptures. In the Bible, Paul writes much about the revelation of God. God reveals Himself through His Word. Paul also mentions that the Bible recognizes evidence of type (1), i.e. the witness of nature (Romans 1).

Man may use both types of evidence, that of nature and of revelation, to reach firm conclusions about the nature of God and the purpose of human existence. But can he rely on his thought processes in these considerations? Is his brain a reliable instrument in this search for God and for the meaning behind human existence? The answer is, alas—as so often—both yes and no! Paul the apostle often challenges us to reflect, i.e. to think. He demanded concentrated attention from his audience, i.e. careful thought when he spoke of the Messiah (Acts 28:26-27). Thus he reckons that the thought processes must be intrinsically reliable. On the other hand, the same apostle warned specifically against the unreliability of certain types of human thought: "But the natural man receiveth not the things of the Spirit of God: for they are foolishness unto him: neither can he know them because they are spiritually discerned" (1 Cor. 2:14).

So here we have an apparently paradoxical situation. On the one hand, Paul admonishes men and challenges them to think sensibly with him. Thus, he behaves as if men really can safely think. On the other hand, he firmly states that certain people cannot recognize certain things, i.e., they cannot think them out. In the areas in which they cannot think, they no longer possess any capacity to comprehend; they cannot understand. What is the solution to this contradiction?

As so often is the case with problems such as these, deeper knowledge lies under the surface of the difficulties. In several places in the Bible, Paul teaches that human knowledge, human capacity for thought and human receptive ability are not static, but dynamic factors. In principle, most people are capable of thinking problems through, aided by their ratio, until they reach a conclusion. This capacity is like computer capacity and depends on the brain's wiring.

If, however, a person with his thinking apparatus comes to a conclusion which requires action, then he has two alternatives. Either he can obey the intelligent decision which he reached by valid thought processes, or he can refuse to obey it—for an intellectual decision does not, of course, of itself alter or determine a person's way of life. What a person does with the intellectual decision, how he handles it and acts upon it, that is quite a different matter.

The two processes together—the thinking and the obeying of thought decisions—these intellectual decisions and actions condition a person's conscience and therefore character. The conscience needs intellectual enlightenment by the thought processes. But if a person obeys the demands of his conscience which has been enlightened by intelligent thought, he becomes filled with joy and his thought processes can further enlighten his conscience regarding other problems. If, however, he does not obey the demands of his conscience, then (1) his conscience is injured, scarred, and hardened. Thus the basis of his inner voice will be lost. But a second process occurs simultaneously with the hardening of his conscience; (2) the reasoning processes, the ratio, the thought processes which led to the enlightenment of his conscience, become darkened. The person suffering from a hardened conscience will no more be able to discern. He will be able to develop less ratio in that area. His thought processes become dulled, together with his conscience. Thus, conscience and the thought processes which condition knowledge (and conscience) are dynamic and not static factors.

It is important to realize that not only the Bible teaches this dynamic view of the thought processes and of the conscience. Our daily experience in life has taught us just the same, for if a criminal commits his first murder, his conscience and also his ratio (reasoning power) suffer extensively. But after he has killed another twenty victims, his conscience is hardened. Many such people even then begin to justify their murders with their thought processes! The murders serve the cause of freedom, of revolution, or even of human good! In their inner selves they know very well that violence and murder solve no problems. But in order to silence the accusations of their conscience, they begin to rationalize and to justify their misdeeds. Thus, their conscience becomes dulled and their capacity for cool and rational thought slowly or quickly is lost.

The human capacity for conviction and thought persuasion thus depends on a delicate, sensitive mechanism, which can easily be damaged by misuse. Examples of such abuse are not difficult to find. Under Hitler certain SS men killed their prisoners "like flies." They had ditches dug, then lined up the prisoners who had dug the ditches in front of the holes. Thereupon they mowed the prisoners down with machine guns so that they buried themselves. Some commanders enjoyed this spectacle so much that they even had it accompanied by orchestras of prisoners playing Wagner's music! The pleasure obtained by the commanders from these proceedings grew with practice. At first they found these murders revolting. With time they eventually dulled their conscience by misuse and the terror of their deeds caused them less trouble. Finally they enjoyed their rationalized misdeeds. These horrors were even rationalized under the heading of "loyalty to the Fatherland." The functions of the ratio (mind) and the conscience are not static, but dynamic!

When a young biology student hears for the first time from his professor that life and the entire cell originate from stochastic chemical reactions and not from any extra-material planning or concept, he is usually intellectually shocked and even horrified. He thinks of the structure of the eye, the liver, the bee orchid, or of a virus. His ratio (mind) rebels against being taught that structure, concepts, machines, language, code, information, and projects originate from stochastic (random) phenomena. He knows that this contradicts experimental experience. Never did any machine develop spontaneously from any inorganic matter. He comes to this conclusion simply because so much speaks for the planning of all biological and other machines by a creator. This thought process now registers with his conscience. He must therefore act and own up to the fact that he cannot and indeed will not believe this biological chance, Darwinian nonsense.

Yet, at the same time he knows that he must pass his exams. His professor is likely to fail him if there is any suspicion that he does not conform to evolutionary theory. So the student under pressure denies the insight of his thought processes and rational mind, thus injuring his conscience. He joins in the chorus with everyone else, intoning that stochastic phenomena created the super-machine we call the biological cell. Thus he claims that the greatest reduction of entropy and indeed the most sublime order or machine ever seen by the world—namely, man and the human brain—developed with no plan and with no concept of any sort. By this means he denies not only his own rationality and common sense, but at the same time his Creator too, by willingly believing nonsense. In this manner the mass hysteria we mentioned previously develops. Finally, he is no longer able to recognize the fact that this position represents an unconscionable misuse of the function of the thought processes lent him by his Creator for use and not for abuse. Conscience and the ability to reason have thus both been injured by doing despite to reason in the interest of conformity and personal advancement.

Soon it becomes impossible to converse with him seriously on the subject without causing anger. He can no longer talk in an unprejudiced manner in this whole area of thought . . . without emotions being unpleasantly aroused. Those who disagree with him and do insist on reasoning will be eliminated by denigration. Soon he may ask with Pilate: "What is truth?" (John 18:38), even though the truth is looking right into his brain. By lack of courage or weakness of the will there was insufficient determination to follow the demands of plain rational thought processes, insight, and common sense which results in damaging both the conscience and the thought processes. Even the apostle Paul said that men were "without [rational] excuse" if they denied the testimony of their Creator in the testimony of all nature (Rom. 1). Functional damage of this type both in the conscience and in the thought processes is surely manifest in many of the symptoms shown by modern society. How much of this may be due to evolutionary teaching in modern schools and universities?

Let us risk summarizing some of these thoughts with a simple allegory. The human brain can be compared with a coffee mill. Given good coffee beans, it produces good, refreshing, stimulating coffee. But if small round pebbles, instead of coffee beans, are fed into the mill, the mill will be damaged and at the same time produce no coffee at all. The human brain is the coffee mill, which gladly grinds facts, theses, dissertations, and ideas like coffee beans. The "coffee" (conclusions, understanding, theses) thus produced refreshes us. If, however, a man feeds his "coffee mill" (brain) with impossible "facts," theses, dissertations, and ideas, with "artifacts" (i.e., with "stones") and pseudoscience, the brain (his "coffee mill") will be functionally damaged—and that man does not receive the "coffee" (understanding) that he requires . . . he is deprived of coherent, sensible theses on the meaning of life and the purpose of our human existence, becoming thereby frustrated.

In order to regain our lost purpose in life and to dispel the modern frustrations of meaningless life, we urgently need the courage of our convictions to obey the religious, scientific, and philosophical conclusions reached by our reasonable thought. A Creator does exist! We must openly stand by this fact. And this Creator purchased our redemption and reconciliation with Himself through Christ's death and resurrection. If we openly stand by this fact, our conscience and also our understanding will both flourish. As a result we will experience Him in our hearts in the Christian rebirth. Thus the long-yearned-for fellowship between man and his God will be reestablished, and thus do we begin to regain by stages paradise lost.

BOOK TWO

Is This a God of Love?

By A.E. Wilder-Smith

Contents

CHAPTER

1

The Pink Professor

When I was a student of natural sciences in England, some of our lectures were given by a professor who had marked leftist tendencies. His lectures at the university were the poorest we ever endured. He'd bring a load of scientific journals into the lecture hall, open them, apparently at random, and then just talk. But he was a gentleman and was kind, in his reserved way, to all of us.

A complete transformation took place in the evenings when he went into town and stood on a soapbox to harangue the masses with the verve and skill of the convinced revolutionary. He was nobly rewarded by his leftist political friends when they gained control of the country, for he soon became a peer with the title of "lord" and was appointed an important administrator of a big university.

This professor was—in common with many Marxist theorists—a convinced and militant atheist. One day he came into the laboratory, unnoticed by me, as I was talking to another student about things other than purely materialistic science. I remarked that, not surprisingly, the study of matter would probably yield information only about matter. Trans-material matters might exist, but they would be overlooked by such methods. One could not expect to pick up ultraviolet light with a film sensitive only to infrared light. But even if infrared paper showed nothing, that would not prove that no ultraviolet wavelengths existed. I saw no reason not to believe in God merely because our instruments had not detected Him. Perhaps they were not on the same wavelength.

Overhearing these remarks, our professor exploded. "It really is a mystery to me," he said, "how otherwise intelligent people can say they believe in any god, let alone in a good and wise One whom they call a Person. We can explain the whole universe and all of life without resorting to the outdated and unnecessary postulate of a god behind it all. Chance and long time spans will do all that your theologians imagine He did without ever appealing to such nonsense as the 'Old Man in the Skies.'"

He continued: "It really is beyond my comprehension that intelligent people today could still be taken in by the same old drivel. I can understand cannibals in the jungle talking as you do. But not a student of the natural sciences in the twentieth century. It is bad enough to have people believing theoretically in a god behind things. But you people are much worse. You believe you have a personal sort of friendship with this God of yours and think you will therefore get preferential treatment from Him. I can understand, perhaps, some old people saying they believe in some sort of mysterious Spirit when they see a sunrise, a beautiful face, a rose or an orchid. But it is proof of positive lack in intelligence on the part of those same people when they do not take the time to see the other side of the coin. They have not the courage to see the other side and boldly throw out their mythical gods—the cowards!"

Having switched into his soapbox mood, our professor was in dead earnest—and angry! "People must be lacking in I.Q. if they do not see the other side of the picture which wipes out all the sunset and beauty stuff." He continued by talking about the cat stalking the mouse and playing with it, letting it totter away half dead and then grabbing it again at the last minute in its horrible claws. Then, when the poor mouse did not have the strength to provide any more fun for the cat, it would squeeze the life out of its tattered body, biting its head off with a juicy crunch, and purring with delight at the evening's entertainment. "It is marvelous that your intelligent, almighty, all-loving and kind God prepared both the mouse in its helplessness and the cat with its talon strength and cruel mentality. This is a beautiful proof of the goodness of your God," he said, with a look of profound scorn in my direction.

I shrank into my corner of the laboratory, but he had not finished with me. "What about the young mother dying of cancer, her body stinking of decay before they take the baby from her and put her in her coffin? Is that your proof of the great Creator who made all things well — 'all things bright and beautiful. The Lord God made them all'?" he hissed. "And what about your capitalists who have worn down the working masses for centuries and built your churches to help you do it? We are going to alter all that — and quickly, believe me!"

"What disgusts me," he said, "is the rank hypocrisy of it all." After a pause to regain his poise, he added, "What about all the agony — the agony of the father and children left behind when they bury the mother? What about the lifetimes of hunger suffered by the poor in India and Russia? Did your good God create all that as well as the sunrises and the laughing faces?" Looking grimly at me, he leaned across the table and said slowly, "Because, if He did — if He did make the disgusting, the cruel and the nauseating as well as the beautiful — then I, for one, would believe Him to be a devil and not a god. Only a devil could make the apparently beautiful and then mock us all with the anguish of the disgusting. But, as I am not so medieval as to believe either in devils or gods, for that matter, I regard the whole argument as a pure wanton waste of time, not worthy of mention in a scientific laboratory."

Having unburdened his soul, he regained some of his professorial aplomb and smilingly looked around for any answers that might be forthcoming. I mumbled something to the effect that his was only one side of the question. Other great people had no difficulty in maintaining an entirely opposite view.

"Let us leave out the question of wars and suffering caused by man himself," he said. "We might explain problems caused by man directly as due to his not being evolved far enough away from his animal ancestors. If we wait long enough, he will evolve higher and get better. Let us leave that and look at another field to which no one has ever honestly turned with a reply that was satisfactory to me. What about the refinement of torture we see all around us, which has nothing whatever to do with man's nature? Take the designed torture we can all see in the transmission of the malarial parasite. It shows signs of what looks like careful, thoughtful planning with the single purpose of plaguing and torturing the host animal, or man. To me the whole system looks like a remarkable sort of planning, if a good god worked it all out. As I said before, if you want a plan behind the universe and life, this sort of setup and planning seems to show a good and a bad, a kindly and a vindictive planner all in one—a god who is a devil."

Musing, he continued, "No, I just cannot believe this religious stuff myself. It really is just too ridiculous. My intelligence and my common sense force me to reject the whole bag of nonsense. I am near enough to being a nihilist, you tell me. But I should become an absolute nihilist if I were to force myself to believe in a god who is a devil. An almighty God, such as you believe in, and a good God, just could not show so many evidences of what appear to be thoughtful, planned goodness, such as sunrises and other beauties, and at the same time so many signs of cold, calculated, intelligent sadism. If you were able to develop sufficient logic," he said, scornfully addressing himself directly to me, "you would have recognized long ago that your views lead directly to nihilism. Can you imagine any supreme, almighty, personal being, who was at the same time all-wise and all-good and yet frightfully vindictive and bad, planning all sorts of plagues and diseases as well as the beauty of the rising sun and the healthy body? It just does not make sense. It is plain bunk." He turned from me in contempt.

There was quiet for a short while. Then he began once more: "Of course, you people always try to get around the difficulty by actually assuming a devil, who surprised the all-knowing and all-powerful, almighty One by upsetting His apple cart when He was not looking. I suppose you attribute the disease, cancer, war, exploitation of the workers, and all the rest of this world's woes to a devil, do you not? But do you not realize that if God were almighty and good, wishing us—the so-called creatures of His hand—well, He must have neutralized the machinations of your devil before he got to work with his hosts of wicked angels in which you, no doubt, believe? Then the devil could not have been a source of devilry, could he? Of course, if your God is not almighty with respect to the devil, then there is only one thing to say about Him: He is not God at all any more. So you destroy Him this way if you do not destroy Him the other way. If God cannot get even with the devil, then the devil must be God too; and we are once more reduced to the primitive ideas of warring gods and devils in heaven and hell. You are not suggesting that we revert to ideas like that, are you? They held up intellectual progress and emancipation for centuries. I shall consider you an enemy of all true progress if you have the effrontery to inform me in a scientific laboratory that you believe in that sort of trash," he said, looking hard at me.

I am afraid most of us were rather like the proverbial rabbit when confronted by the snake—transfixed. No answers seemed to be able to formulate themselves in our brains. After all, our professor was a learned man. He was not just repeating slogans learned in Marxist circles. Obviously he was thoroughly convinced of his views. His extreme seriousness made him willing to stand up on a soapbox and confront the mob—an act which must have been rather humiliating for a professor of his standing. Although he was almost useless as a professor and lecturer in the classroom and experimental laboratory, we respected him as a man, even though not all of us liked his convictions on political or religious matters.

While we were thinking about these things, he quietly started again. "I used to say," he continued, "that I was an agnostic and therefore could say nothing for certain about religious matters. But now that I am getting more mature and experienced, I have come to the conclusion that I am in reality a total atheist. I have been forced to the point where I do not believe in any god, either good or bad. That is, I believe neither in a good god nor in a bad devil. Such beliefs raise more difficulties than they remove. They just complicate matters. So today I just leave religious matters outside my realm of thought—like alchemy. And I do not like people raising them in the classroom either. They only confuse, being highly unscientific and subjective. I do not need to blur my intellectual horizon with such primitive methods of thought any longer. The Marxists are not altogether wrong when they call religion "opium for the people." It is just that; it muddles their thoughts, blurs their vision and, because they can see clearly no more, renders them an easy prey for the capitalists who are just waiting to exploit them for their own benefit."

THE SPOKESMAN OF MANY THINKING PEOPLE

I have never forgotten that afternoon in the laboratory. Certainly our professor had thought more about these matters than we students had. Moreover, he understood the problems of the ordinary thinking men and, when he wished, could be an excellent spokesman for them. Because he understood them, he could sway them when he spoke. He never spoke with such conviction on cold, matter-of-fact chemical matters, but no one could get across ideas like he when revolution and Marxism came up. His attitudes are still typical of many university professors all over the West. Since the total collapse of Marxism behind the former iron curtain there are many professors in the East who have abandoned the views of our pink professor for the simple reason that they work neither economically nor socially.

The subject raised that afternoon in the laboratory is the very question occupying the minds of many thinking people in the West today. It looms large in the life of the person who, though satiated with life's material goods and apparently concerned only with pleasure and prosperity, is brought face to face with life's cruelties and suffering every day in his newspaper and on radio and television news, and is jolted by what is happening around him in his own life. If God is almighty—and if He is God, He must be almighty—why doesn't He stop all this chaos, all these wars, all the unrighteousness, injustice, misery and suffering in this world? Why did He ever let them start? Mere men everywhere are bending all their efforts to do what they can to stop it all. But, fortunately or unfortunately, men are not almighty and therefore cannot reach their goal.

Years ago, a student friend crippled with polio told me, "If you want me to believe in your God, I shall expect Him first of all to make a better job of the world we live in—and of me." I spent a good deal of time with him and he was apparently glad to listen to me. In my student enthusiasm I explained not only the Christian way of salvation by Christ's works but also the intricacies of prophecy and the end of the age. Afterward he turned to me and said that now that he knew the way, he didn't need to do anything about it. For when he saw the end coming, he would quickly accept God's way and be all right forever! A year or two later he was stricken with a stroke one Sunday morning while shaving. He died in seconds, without a sound. His wife found him an hour or so later.

If God loves us men and women, as the Bible assumes He does, why doesn't He end all misery and immediately set up a workable, orderly system such as most people of good will would like and for which they are striving? Doesn't He care for us any longer? If He doesn't care and has forgotten us, why should we care about Him? Because He has allowed evil to exist along with good, thus apparently compromising Himself in His omnipotence, many thinking people despair of an answer, or become atheists, just as my professor had done.

THE PROBLEM IS NOT NEW

Before further consideration of this question, we must remind ourselves that it is by no means new. Some have the mistaken idea that they are very modern if they handle the question as my professor did. They think that it stamps them as being advanced thinkers in having recognized that mankind is facing a new problem—and that they have solved it in a particularly new way.

Of course, this is not the case. When thistles and thorns sprang up after mankind's first couple had fallen from the paradise of God by disobedience, they probably asked the same sort of question. Why indeed did God allow all this? Does He no longer love us and care for us? It looks as if He does not, for the very ground we cultivate does not bring forth its harvest anymore. The birth of Cain was probably accomplished by pain, which was capped when he became his brother's murderer. How can that grisly history coincide with God's goodness and omnipotence?

Job could have asked the same kind of questions when the messengers came to him, one after another, each reporting a worse catastrophe to his family. It got so bad that Job cursed the day he had been born. He lost everything, including his health. Even his wife deserted him, telling him to curse God and die. How could Job believe in a holy, perfect and omnipotent God, concerned about him and his family, when all the catastrophes about him pointed in the opposite direction? He is God. He could have stopped it if He had wanted to. Did He want to find a way out for Job? And, if not, was He a sadist? Did He still care about Job in allowing all this to happen to the poor innocent man? The testimony of God and man was that Job was perfect—and innocent. Yet it all happened, and no explanation was forthcoming—except that good Job praised God for having given and then taken away again. No real answer was forthcoming until right at the end of the book. If God did not care about poor, innocent, perfect Job, why should Job love God? Of course, God cared for Job in a way which had never occurred to Job. God justified Job before all heaven by demonstrating Job's steadfastness under duress.

It is true, of course, that there was still a great deal in Job and Adam's worlds which pointed to God's care in spite of thorns and thistles and catastrophes. But it is also true that there is just as much in our world. At the beginning of Adam's career the picture pointing to God's care and love was clear. In that earlier world, everything indicated only God's care and omnipotence. Many things now pointed away from this direction, and the area of God's order had retreated into quite a minute spot on the stage of life. So the same sort of contradictions arose in Adam and Job's times as they do now. Thus the problem is by no means new. It is as old as mankind.

Accordingly, the question presents itself as follows: Why should we be asked to believe and trust in a good God, thereby flying in the face of all — or at least a good deal of — the contemporary evidence? One physicist put it as follows: Why does God value faith in Him so much as to make it the very condition, according to the Christian way of life, of entry into His kingdom? It seems most unfair to me. For faith means believing right in the face of contradictory evidence. Faith to me is merely the result of forcing myself to believe and trust in God's goodness and care when a goodly part of the evidence on hand leads me to reject such a trust. Most preachers seem to preach faith as though it were the faculty of believing something which is not true — forcing oneself to believe and act in spite of evidence to the contrary. Why should God value a faith which acts against all common sense and evidence? Such action short-circuits one of our highest faculties: the ability to weigh evidence and then act on it. Faith believes what it cannot see; it accepts evidence it cannot weigh. Why should God make as a condition for entering His presence and kingdom our ability to short circuit, abuse and render null and void the very logic and evidence-weighing faculty with which the Bible says He endowed us? God gave us logical ability. Why does He demand that we act and think illogically in faith as a condition of entering His kingdom?"

To return to our first line of approach to this problem, then, the question is: If the same Being planned both the good and the bad, the beautiful and the ugly, the sadistic and the loving, then does all serious, logical, reasoning thought about Him become impossible with our thinking faculties?

ANOTHER APPROACH

What does the Bible teach about this apparent state of illogic? Remarkably enough, neither the New nor the Old Testament sees any illogic in the situation! For example, in Romans 1, which deals with this question in detail, Paul the apostle teaches in a clear and uncompromising manner that creation doesn't show the slightest sign of contradiction in these matters. It gives only one plain line of thought—that the whole creation reveals that God is a glorious, omnipotent Creator—and nothing else. Paul says, "Because that which may be known of God is manifest in them; for God has shown it unto them. For the invisible things of Him from the creation of the world are clearly seen, being understood by the things that are made (nature), even His eternal power and Godhead; so that they are without excuse."[1]

Thus the Bible teaches, as do many ancient sources, that when a man regards nature he is seeing as in a mirror the Creator. The Bible doesn't ignore the apparent problems of war, disease, poverty, pain and chaos. It says quite a lot about these subjects and even suggests cures for some of them. But it does not see them in the light in which my professor saw them. The Bible does not think that these things cloud the issue about the Creator, as do many thinking people. Rather, it teaches that the person who regards nature as it is today and does not see the power of a glorious, invisible Godhead in nature—with no clouding of the issue by the mixture of good and evil we all see—that person is "without excuse" for not believing! This is surely a rather strong pill to the modern intellectual who pleads intellectual difficulties for his disbelief in God.

Adding insult to injury, the Bible goes one step further in teaching that not only should a person see the Godhead, the glorious Creator, when he sees mixed nature, but seeing it he should be filled with thanks to God, glorifying Him for revealing His wisdom and power in the creation. So, apparently I should have told my professor that he was not only "without excuse" but also a "thankless" person—if I had been ready to give him a biblical view of himself. Somehow, I don't think he would have appreciated that! Certainly, at that time I did not have the necessary maturity to say such a thing without causing a major incident, and a lot of misunderstanding.

Paul continues the argument by maintaining that a sense of wonder and reverence should fill every observer of the present confused creation. Offsetting this wonder should be a sense of our own vanity and foolishness, pervading us and all who do not see the creation in this light. Finally, all these feelings on observing God's handiwork should make the observer a worshiper. If I had told my professor that he had all the evidence necessary to make him fall on his knees and worship God, undoubtedly he would have thought me a lunatic.

But Paul insists that if those reactions to the creation don't take place in us, we are abusing our reasoning powers. As a consequence of this abuse we shall become totally unable, in the course of time, to use our higher reasoning faculties and logical powers. Paul expresses this thought by saying our "heart" will become "darkened" and our "imagination" will become "vain." Also, he maintains that under such circumstances even sexual morality will die in us. Men will begin to sexually abuse their own bodies—homosexuality will arise, and normal sex relations will be stifled. Certainly my professor would not have appreciated this step of the argument in the least, for he appeared to be a moral man.

In summary, at least parts of Holy Scripture do not appear to sympathize greatly with the intellectual difficulties discussed here. The Bible says a look at nature should be enough to make a person a convinced, thankful, worshiping believer. The question remains: Why does the Bible take this stand, seeing that at least some thoughtful modern people in the Western world today have found that the observation of the universe has by no means made them worshipers or believers? (Here I am not thinking of Taoists, etc.). On the contrary, those who have studied the universe in the natural sciences and other disciplines have often experienced the most difficulties with respect to worshipping and believing. Indeed, quite a majority have simply turned away from any thought of God.

Investigation of "that which is seen" has not revealed to them the "unseen" but has often turned them from believing in anything divine and invisible. In no way has it made them worshipers of some unseen Being. For what they have perceived shows so many paradoxes and apparent contradictions that, judging the unseen by their perception, it becomes either ridiculous or superfluous for further serious thought.

Some intellectuals conclude that if the seen can give no credible picture of the unseen, being a Christian is synonymous with being a third-rate intellectual. They assume that the Christian is intellectually incapable of comprehending the contradictions and paradoxes inherent in the allegedly rather naive and intellectually impossible Christian faith.

Clearly, the basic difficulty confronting both the Christian and the intellectual in aligning matters of belief with matters of the intellect is intimately tied up with the question of the origin of evil. If we could account for the origin of evil without impugning God's omnipotence, love and holiness, then we would be able to go a long way toward solving these difficulties. A future chapter deals with this basic problem of the origin of evil.

CHAPTER

2

Thought and Action: Today and Yesterday

Few realize how differently people today use the process of thinking as compared to individuals of a hundred years ago. We live in an age of unprecedented technology and, therefore, of technological thought, so of necessity technological subject matter must color today's thought processes more than in the past. However, beyond a mere change of shades of thought, entirely new thought processes or modes have been adopted. Radical changes in the very mechanism of thought have occurred.

LET US REASON

A century ago the average thinking person considered life and the universe to be orderly and contain meaning. He willingly admitted that it was often difficult to discover the meaning and order behind things. But this fact did not disturb him in his basis of thought, namely, that order and meaning were there if he could only find them. Though human stupidity or weakness might distort and slow down the unraveling of meaning, the meaning was still there. The book of the universe and of life was hard to decode or read. But the average thinker was still convinced that it was a code capable of being deciphered if sufficient insight and intelligence could be brought to bear on it.

Based on such premises, huge efforts were easily justified in the quest to decipher the mysteries of the meaning and mechanisms of life and the universe. The overrun from this conviction can be seen today in the momentum still present in such efforts as molecular biology and space exploration where laws, interpretation, and meaning are being sought. However, it is not generally recognized that large areas of today's philosophy, art, music, general culture, and even theology have abandoned the very premises which launched the huge scientific effort which has utterly changed the whole world of technology and science. Most practicing research scientists still work on the premise that nature is a code and that life is a meaningful system governed by law and yielding its meaning to those who try hard and with enough intelligence. But other branches of knowledge such as those mentioned above have more or less arrived at the conclusion that life and the universe are, in the last analysis, absurd and devoid of meaning. Camus is an example of this, for he received the Nobel Prize for saying just this in his own elegant way.

Thus, where our forefathers based their thought processes on the premise that life and the universe were meaningful, thought processes today are governed by exactly the opposite premise. Sartre, Camus and other modern thinkers have obtained the highest praise from today's intelligentsia for elegantly and cleverly conveying the premise that life, man, and the universe are meaningless. It naturally follows, therefore, that suffering is meaningless too.

Only in such a cultural atmosphere were scientific theories as those of Darwin able to take root and flourish both in scientific and popular circles. For Darwin, aided by Huxley, propagated the view, using mountains of scientific detail as evidence, that all life processes arose spontaneously, without motivation or rationale, from randomness. In the last analysis, randomness is congruent with lack of order and, therefore, with lack of meaning. According to this view, the mixtures of amino acids that are supposed to have given spontaneous birth to life showed no meaning or motivation behind them. No volition guided these and other building blocks into the codes of meaning that make up DNA as we know it today. The first nucleic acids and proteins allegedly arose spontaneously from meaninglessness. This boils down to saying that if there is any meaning in life or its origin at all, that meaning must be based on sheer meaninglessness. The same applies to life's destiny—it must be meaningless too.

EQUATING FACT TO NON-FACT

Thus, biological sciences are also mixed up in the changes in thought processes, which have so radically altered the modern world. Consider the lengths to which scientific philosophers such as Sir Julian Huxley have gone. He teaches all who will listen that human and social order flourish better if humans believe in a god or support some sort of religion, for their belief helps them respect each other. Therefore, he advocates the propagation of some sort of belief in a god external to nature, even though he says that we, the enlightened ones, well know that such a belief does not correspond to the actual facts of nature but is thoroughly false and deceptive. "Religion today is imprisoned in a theistic frame of ideas," he claims, "compelled to operate in the unrealities of the dualistic world. In the unitary humanistic frame it acquires a new look and new freedoms. With the aid of our new vision it has the opportunity of escaping from the theistic impasse and of playing its proper role in the real world of unitary existence."[1]

Schaeffer rightly observes: "Now it may be true that it can be shown by observation that society copes better with life through believing that there is a god. But in that case, surely optimistic humanism is being essentially unreasonable . . . if, in order to be optimistic, it rests upon the necessity of mankind believing and functioning upon a lie."

In other words, human society demonstrably needs to believe in a god to function optimally. "All right," says today's scientific philosopher, "let them carry on with that belief if it helps them function, even though, strictly speaking, it is a lie." Huxley has no objection to believing in anti-facts if that allows man to continue being optimistically humanist.

Consider the chaos implicit in this kind of thought pattern. Huxley is a scientific humanist who believes in unitary existence—no divine existence outside human existence. This means that there is no thought (Descartes' proof of existence) besides human (or possibly animal) thought. Yet, the human thought he uses is calmly allowed to be non-thought, for there is no objection to holding a non-god to be a real god!

Surely everyone, including the rationalist, believes that man is a rational being, and that rationality is a part—an integral part—of every man. To postulate that man, in order to function, must be non-rational will divide and destroy his very being. This is the position to which scientific philosophy in some quarters—and they are influential quarters—has led us. Not only is this the main line in present-day intellectual thought, postulated by gifted intellectuals like Huxley, Camus and Sartre, but Fellini and Antonioni of Italy, Slessinger of England and Bergman of Sweden all actively proclaim the same irrational rationalism in their films. Thus, the view that life is meaningless is not merely the property of the highbrows but is being claimed by so-called lowbrows too. Popular mass education is seeing to this. Nobel Prizes are doled out to those who are responsible for teachings that are destroying rational man!

HOW FAITH IS GAINED

How can one get a man to believe in a non-fact in the same way that our fathers believed in demonstrable facts? That is the grand feat which modern thought has now accomplished with Kierkegaard's aid. A new methodology was developed especially for this one purpose—how to believe in and be convinced of non-facts and make them the basis of our faith.

The pattern is quite simple. If a man can see no rational rhyme, sense nor reason in life and its problems, if he cannot find any way of decoding life's mysteries, then he must no longer seek solutions by rational thought. He must close his eyes, throw life's textbook into the corner, and take a leap of faith based on non-facts. Thus, non-facts are serving the purpose formerly monopolized by facts as a foundation for thought and faith. Theology professors have faith in faith rather than faith in a fact or a person.

It is vitally important to realize how different this method of thought is as compared to that employed by the prophets throughout Holy Scripture. In the Acts of the Apostles,[2] Paul is reported to have reasoned with the elders with tears day and night about matters of faith. He was ready to throw his faith overboard if it did not comply with the known facts. If the body of the Lord Jesus Christ could have been found after His death and resurrection, that one fact would have abolished at one stroke all Christian faith and doctrine forever. For the whole Christian position (faith) turned (and turns) on this one out-standing fact—the Lord rose from the dead as He had promised before His death. His body was transmuted from material mortality to the supramortal—to immortality. The disproving of this one central fact—the pillar of faith, which was attested to by more than five hundred living people at the time Paul wrote of the resurrection—would have destroyed Christianity.

In those days Christians did not arrive at their faith by a leap in the dark but by basing their thought processes—and therefore their faith—on the fact of Christ's resurrection. Any other way of arriving at a real Christian faith stands forever outside the testimony of Scripture as well as that of living Christians.

THE EXASPERATED STUDENT

I once knew a student who disliked higher mathematics yet needed this knowledge to pass examinations. After many futile attempts to master a chapter of a rather abstruse aspect of the subject, he threw the book into the corner of his room, muttering that it was all bunk and nonsense—to him. But it was not nonsense to everyone. For others had mastered the same contents and extracted meaning from them. The difficulty was that the student, being unable to comprehend the message of the abstruse chapter, concluded that it was absurd nonsense. His conclusion was, unfortunately for him, wrong.

Camus and others are saying, in effect, the same thing—life is absurd and meaningless—to them. But other serious people— although usually the first to admit that life's book is hard to decipher—confess to having found satisfying solutions to at least some of life's problems. And their conclusions are based on the facts given by events of history such as the resurrection of Christ. And more and more problems and seeming paradoxes may be resolved into order by the careful and logical application of thought.

THE AGE OF REASON

Our much-prized age of reason has regressed into an age of non-reason. The age of scientific philosophy has reverted to an age of non- or anti-philosophy. What else can we conclude if leaders of modern thought say that they're willing to believe in the existence of a god who they really don't think exists in order to hold onto their optimistic humanism? Learning and philosophy are dependent upon the communication of meaning and message. Is it any wonder that communication between man and man, generation and generation is breaking down because the message of the communication allegedly has been found to be meaningless? In this way philosophy today has become, in fact, an anti-philosophy, just as the age of reason has become an age of unreasonable blind leaps of faith in a pitch black, unreasonable and absurd world—of the kind described by Camus.

The whole situation as seen by our present world philosophy can be well summed up in these lines by Hans Arp, one of the original members of the Dada group:

Francis Schaeffer comments: "On the basis of modern man's methodology, whether expressed in philosophy, art, literature or theology, there can be no other ending than this—man tumbles into the bottomless."[3]

PICASSO IN CHICAGO

Several years ago I was standing in front of the Civic Center in Chicago, where stands a huge abstract sculpture by Picasso for which the mayor of Chicago paid a large sum of money. While I was determining from which angles it would be best to photograph this piece of art, a well-mannered Chicagoan quietly asked why I was going to all this trouble. I said I wanted to get the effect and meaning in real life faithfully reproduced on film. His answer was quite interesting. He said that since in his opinion the work carried and expressed no communicable meaning in real life, it was a waste of time and good film to try and reproduce it in a photo!

ATHEISTIC CLERGYMEN

Picasso again demonstrates the tendency of modern art to detach itself from the realities and facts of modern life and, in doing so, to lose meaning for many people. Theology, the proverbial laggard in modern intellectual activity, has followed philosophy, art and music, albeit at a distance of some years.

I spoke to a young German clergyman recently just before he was to conduct a confirmation service. In all earnestness he informed me that he, as a pastor, believed that there was no God behind the universe, although he would not yet dare to say so openly in his church. He believed in an atheistic theology. Theology being the science of the study of divinity or God, we have arrived at the position of a pastor studying the science of no-God, which we may equate to nothingness, for a god that does not exist is nothing. So the conclusion was that he had spent seven years studying nothingness! I pointed out this rather elementary fact to him. He retreated in some confusion, saying that I had misunderstood him. He did not say, he explained, that he believed in an atheistic theology, but rather in an a-theistic theology. This was quite different, he said, for it meant that he could continue in his theology without God — that is, a-theistically rather than atheistically! One wonders what sort of a shepherd of his flock such a young man will make when he has to comfort the dying and lay hands on the sick and those wracked with pain.

CONSEQUENCES

But why bother to go into all this theory and philosophy? If there is no meaning behind the universe and life, why try to find any?

The reason is simple. Man is a rational being. To ask him to live in and for meaninglessness or non-rationality is to ask him to destroy himself. He goes into despair and will not rest, if he is honest with himself, until he is able to replace meaninglessness with meaning and order.

If contemporary rational thinkers—being rational creatures—
see injustice, suffering, wars, violence and apparent meaninglessness on every side, they cannot rest until they have found a
rationale of some sort for it all. Huxley admits that he is prepared
to be an optimistic humanist on the basis of believing in a non-
existent god—one he knows not to be there, but whose presence
and existence we must postulate to keep ourselves happy. But
the use of a non-rationality, a lie, to keep a man rational and
happy will surely destroy the very basis of rationality!

No, if rational man is to remain rational, he must use *real* fact
to find some meaning for all the apparent chaos and meaninglessness which surround him. How can he rationally explain
a beautiful young mother dying of cancer while her child is
being born? How can he avoid despair on seeing men, women
and children mutilated by war, hunger and pestilence? These
are realities. Camus shrugged his shoulders at such sights, sensitive as he was, and said that the world and life are meaningless jokes—absurd.

Jesus Christ saw similar suffering and spoke of the beggar
Lazarus covered with sores and lying at the rich man's gate. He
had mercy and compassion on the beggar. But He did not leave
it at that and shrug it all off, just as if life and Lazarus were
meaningless victims of a harsh, absurd and cruel world. He
interpreted Lazarus' apparently meaningless suffering—and
the rich man's riches too—and told us in no uncertain terms
in Luke 16:20-25 what they meant.

But today's teachers of Christianity have not given convinc-
ing answers to the modern meaningless theorists, even though
Christ's interpretation of the problem is on hand if they care to

read and digest it. The fact is, of course, that Christ's interpretation of Lazarus' suffering and of other problems involving suffering is not generally accepted today. The real reason for the unwillingness to accept His interpretation is coupled with an unwillingness to accept the full fact and impact of resurrection as evidenced in Christ's own body. If we really believed in Christ's and our own resurrection as unshakable facts, we wouldn't have the slightest difficulty in accepting Christ's interpretation of the mystery or the apparent "meaninglessness" of Lazarus' suffering. We have become so used to equating nonfact with fact that we find it difficult to follow rigidly the logical consequences of believing in a real fact! For in Lazarus' case, the introduction of one overlooked fact—namely, personal resurrection—reduced the hopelessness and meaninglessness of his sufferings to meaningfulness.

Christ, as He explained Lazarus' case, kept steadily before Him the fact of personal resurrection. To the humanist bystander tied up in Huxley's idea about "unitary existence," Lazarus as he lay there full of sores was a senseless cruelty, an example of callous torture of innocent humanity. But if the promise of recompense and correction—actually, the mighty recompense of resurrection—is a fact, then of course meaninglessness resolves itself to meaning. For surely, if a short term of suffering is the method by which eternal non-suffering or bliss is to be attained, then Lazarus was in for a bargain—to put it mildly—and reasonableness is restored to apparent unreasonableness.

What modern philosophers have been busy doing—indeed philosophers of all time have practiced the same art—is removing by unbelief certain facts from the sad case of this suffering world, facts given us by God Himself to enable us to handle the problem intellectually. Just as the addition of an overlooked fact (resurrection) brought meaning into the meaninglessness in the case of Lazarus' suffering, so the removal of some fact will reduce it from rationality and meaning to irrationality and meaninglessness. We interpret and diagnose on the basis of all the facts of a case; that is, we appoint meaning in the light of all relevant facts. But remove the facts, even the revealed facts of the Bible, and meaninglessness and inability to diagnose the case must result because the resulting picture is incomplete.

MAN CANNOT LIVE WITHOUT RATIONALITY

It is obviously useless to argue reasonably with anyone who does not believe in meaning, and, therefore, in reason. Many modern theologians and philosophers are in just this position. But this is not the case with a majority of the younger generation. Young people—perhaps firm believers in Camus and Sartre—are finding that they cannot help falling in love with one another, just as their forefathers did. Girls are still pretty and boys still attracted to their beauty of body and psyche. They become aware that the remarkable fact of falling in love with each other, in spite of what they have learned about the absurdity of everything, is not so absurd. Love is a new, hitherto neglected fact and it transforms their lives, giving them purpose where they had imagined there was none. The addition of one fact—human love is a fact and not a nonfact—to their lives has resolved some of life's meaninglessness to meaning.

The fact of love had been overlooked, but now it must be taken into account in the formula for life, just as in the case of Lazarus the resurrection completely altered the equation.

The fact of love brings new rationality and new meaning, just as other facts—beauty in nature, order in the biological cell, chemical laws in biochemistry and electromagnetic laws in valency—help us to see order where previously, without knowledge of these facts, meaninglessness reigned.

IS THERE A PLACE FOR BLIND FAITH?

Someone will be sure to object to this kind of presentation, saying that, after all, the heavy emphasis on reason and rationality excludes the exercise of real faith as the evidence of things not seen but hoped for.

This kind of objection would be valid if one believed that reason is faith. But we have not said that. We have said that evidence and facts should lead to faith and that non-facts should not. To build faith on a sound basis we must have sound facts and not flabby non-facts or meaninglessness. When the facts of a case have been established beyond doubt—for example, that Christ did, as a historical fact, rise from the dead on the third day—then we can start building faith on that fact. For, by being resurrected after death, as He had promised before dying, He proved that He had knowledge which ordinary mortals do not possess about the after-death state. In fact, the predicted and fulfilled resurrection proves that He had divine foreknowledge, and His words bore the weight attributable to divinity. If His words on resurrection have thus been proved to be divine, then surely what He says about me, my death and my resurrection by His power will be divine. These divine facts and words allow me sufficient basis on which to build my faith by trusting in and acting on them. This kind of building on divine evidence and facts, this trusting of them and their Author, is nothing less and nothing more than biblical faith.

All that this really means is that we are objecting to blind faith—leaps in the dark. I am well aware that at times I have no facts or evidence to build upon—probably as Lazarus had no evidence as he lay in misery. I am completely at sea in regard to faith and belief in those difficult situations when I do not know where I am nor what I should do or think. And I am often in that anguished position.

But it is when I am in such deep waters that I take a new look at the facts of divine illumination, help, and guidance which I have previously experienced. Looking back, I see how God has kept His good hand over me, even in allowing apparent catastrophes. Recalling past facts and evidence, I base my faith for the future on them and so reestablish trust for the present where I cannot yet see the needed evidence. But I cannot base trust on nothing, meaninglessness or nothingness. I cannot leap in the dark. I trusted Him in the past; He helped. Is that not fact and evidence that the same will be true of the present and the future, even in ultimate catastrophe? These facts strengthen me to trust Him, the great personal Fact, now, where I see no evidence. Such faith is by no means blind. It is based on a hindsight experience of Him, on facts and on reason. On this basis we treat the problem of suffering.

CHAPTER

3

The Atheistic and Agnostic Positions

Are there any really irreconcilable intellectual difficulties involved in believing in God, or are they only imaginary when carefully examined? I don't believe the ancients were on a lower intellectual plane than we moderns. Even though we have excelled them in technology, we see no evidence of intellectual lethargy on their part. Yet, perhaps a considerable percentage of them believed that the universe showed God's handiwork, whereas most moderns do not.

This difference in approach is not in any way a reflection on the total intellectual capacity of either the moderns or the ancients. Rather, it is a reflection of the increasing mass of knowledge with which every human being in every succeeding generation has to contend. An ancient could have been a master of all that was then known in the combined fields of physics, chemistry, mathematics, geometry, medicine, biology and algebra. Today the mass of knowledge is so great that no human brain can possibly cope with even a fraction of it. Therefore, a fragmentation of knowledge has occurred. But this massive increase has tended to take place in the watertight compartments of the various disciplines into which knowledge has become divided in order to fit the capacity of single brains. The result is that a synthesis of all modern knowledge is rapidly becoming less and less possible. This perfectly natural tendency has had some far-reaching consequences which must be examined before we consider the question of the origin of evil, since the two problems belong together.

Just over a century ago, Darwin, Wallace and Huxley propounded the view that long time spans and chance reactions, coupled with natural selection, would account for all visible living nature without the necessity of involving the volition of any divinity. Huxley thought he could prove this with his appeal to probability laws and his famous six monkeys typing at random for millions of years on six typewriters. The mathematical formulae for the possibility of this view were bandied around and the principle was accepted as true. The natural and logical consequence of the view was that the postulate of divinity behind nature was rendered superfluous from a mathematical point of view. Immense time spans plus chance and natural selection would do all the work hitherto attributed to

God. Thus the world of science became a realm depending on chance as a direct result of the views of these men who believed their conclusions were mathematically well founded. Thus, so called science was believed to have shown that there was no place for the God-postulate. As we shall see there is no scientifically founded reason for accepting this view.

The patient work of scientists simultaneously competent in several disciplines has been necessary to show that Darwin's and Huxley's basic assumptions were chemically, mathematically and biologically untenable.[1] The vastness of today's scientific knowledge makes it obvious that it is a rare scientist who is able to do original work in all these fields simultaneously. As a result, until recently no synthesis between the various fields had been achieved. Instead, watertight compartmentalization had developed. Biologists were unable to test the mathematics of the problem in hand and chemists could not critically assess the biologists' work.

The biologists announced with all due thunder that they could replace God with chance and long timespans plus natural selection. But no mathematicians sufficiently versed in chemistry and biology were forthcoming to assess what the biologists were shouting about. As a result, one discipline, in this case biology, has been building on false chemical, thermodynamic and mathematical premises. The author has written elsewhere of the catastrophic development of this kind of compartmentalization of science.[2]

Because in ancient times learned men possessed a good overall view on life they could believe what the apostle Paul said about the universe demonstrating the nature of the Godhead. It agreed with what they knew about mathematics and biology.

What is generally not realized is that modern man could believe, as did the ancients, that the universe shows God's nature—and still remain within the bounds of modern scientific knowledge—if his knowledge had not become so great that it had to be wrongly compartmentalized. For when the various compartments are carefully examined, the fact emerges that each still speaks one language today, as it did thousands of years ago: that "the heavens declare the glory of God," in spite of the mixture of good and bad.[3]

So we can believe in a good, loving, personal, holy and compassionate God behind it all. But what about evil? Is He the Author of that too? The *Koran* teaches that God made "the mischief of creation," too.[4] Is God the Author of the mixed picture?

THE GOTHIC CATHEDRAL

Before the Second World War, I often visited the huge and beautiful Gothic cathedral at Cologne on the Rhine in Germany. I used to admire this fine example of the architecture of many hundred years ago, with its graceful flying buttresses, a superb high-domed roof, its famous two towers and the medieval stained glass windows.

The more I admired the cathedral, the more I found myself admiring the architects and masons who had originated the whole structure. Over the centuries they had patiently planned and built. All the graceful lines and sturdy foundations had obviously been carefully planned by experts possessing sound knowledge of building mathematics and mechanics as well as a keen appreciation of how to combine both to produce a beautiful total edifice.

That it had so well withstood the ravages of the centuries showed that the workmen and designers not only understood the principles behind beauty, but also those of ensuring endurance. Their craftsmanship was first class in every way. Thus I found myself admiring our forefathers as I admired their workmanship. Considering that they had few of the mechanical devices a modern architect would consider essential for constructing such a masterpiece, the masons and architects of that day certainly did work wonders.

The structure of that cathedral, centuries after it had been built, showed without the slightest doubt something of the mind or minds behind it. Its very compact and organized design made one wonder what sort of drawing offices the builders had at their disposal and how they made their blueprints. To imagine that such a well-conceived edifice simply arose without enormous planning effort would be to invite the just derision of anyone remotely familiar with the construction industry. Even calculations of the various strengths of the construction materials had to be made with old-fashioned arithmetic and not just handed over to a computer. Thus, an almost flawless work showed sharply the minds and hands of its creators. But the picture did not always remain as clear.

COMPLICATING THE ISSUE

During the war, Cologne suffered perhaps the most intensive air bombardment of any city in Western Europe. Reportedly, bombs fell on approximately every two square yards of the entire inner city. Now the cathedral stands almost directly in the railway station yard. Cologne is an important rail center where many lines meet, particularly those connected with the huge and concentrated Ruhr industrial area. Naturally, the allies bombed the railroad yards on many occasions and, not surprisingly, many bombs missed their mark and destroyed nearby housing and property. A number of heavy bombs hit the cathedral, causing immense damage.

In the fall of 1946 when I returned to Germany for the first time after the war, I was greatly dismayed at the sight of the cathedral. It seemed symbolic of the rest of Europe and her spirit. Almost irreparable damage had been done in five years of combat. However, as I approached, the two famous towers were still visible through the morning mist.

Practically every building in the vicinity was razed to the ground; the cathedral alone stood majestically in the midst of the carnage. Coming nearer, however, I could see huge, gaping holes in the sides of the two towers. The holes revealed the massiveness of the masonry, for any other building receiving glancing blows from such high-explosive bombs would have collapsed entirely. But the cathedral, though badly damaged, was not destroyed. Hundreds of tons of concrete and bricks had been used to plug a huge hole high up in one tower, partially replacing the ancient masonry which had been blasted away by an aerial bomb.

The ancient roof was indescribably damaged. Huge rafters and beams, once the cathedral's glory, hung perilously down over the bomb-pocked floor. As the wind blew through the wreckage, small bits and pieces fell to the ground, building up the piles of rubble. A hole marked the place where the organ had once pealed out its accompaniment to worship.

This miserable piece of chaos made a deep impression on me as I stood in the same place where I had once admired the order and beauty of the original edifice. As those memories of former beauty passed through my mind, one idea never even occurred to me. Never did I connect the chaos of the formerly beautiful cathedral with any inefficiency or designed purpose on the part of the constructing architects or masons! They had not built it for such maltreatment.

Similarly, I never began to doubt the existence of the men who designed and constructed the cathedral simply because I could now see so many contradictions in their handiwork. The place was a ruin. But in its ruination it still bore the marks of design. In fact, its design and original beauty were even more emphasized in some respects. For the huge gaping holes in the walls revealed the excellent construction even better than did the remaining undamaged walls. There was no fill or rubbish behind false walls; it was all solid handiwork built to last for centuries. The mighty flying buttresses were still there; the graceful Gothic arches were still standing. But the solid design which was built into the parts of the construction normally hidden from view was now laid bare for all to see how well these craftsmen had done their job.

In summary, even the general ruin and chaos showed (1) the existence and (2) the excellent work of both architects and craftsmen. Furthermore, the ruined structure itself showed in some ways even better than the intact one the existence and skill of the originators. In fact, the whole picture reminded me of the purpose of dissection in learning the anatomy of animals, men and plants. In order to see the order—and beauty—of some aspects of biology, the destroyed or dissected animal or plant serves better than the intact one. The cathedral had certainly been dissected, and its entrails laid bare.

INEFFICIENT ARCHITECTS?

Obviously, no one was going to accuse the architects and craftsmen of designing and building a ruin. The cathedral had been constructed to last—almost forever. Something had happened to it which had not been planned or even conceived of. And yet, even in its ruination, it was generally quite easy to distinguish between the unplanned ruin and the actual architecture. The cathedral at the same time displayed both perfection and ruination—chaos and order mixed up inextricably with one another, just as the world around us presents a picture full of good and evil, beauty and ugliness, order and chaos, love and hate. No one in his right mind ought to deny that life as we see it is a hopeless hodgepodge of such ingredients. However, we should remember that it would be just as illogical to say that the mixed picture of the cathedral proves there was no architect behind it as to say that the ruined, mixed picture of life we see round about us proves that there is no God behind it. My professor, rightly seeing the hodgepodge before him, concluded that therefore,

1. The edifice of creation has neither mind or architect behind it. The atheist maintains that because he sees nothing but

contradictions in nature, therefore there is no God or mind behind it. The Germans call this a *Denkfehler*, a short-circuit in the logic of thinking. And so it is. But it is one seldom seen through today.

2. No characteristics of a mind behind nature can be distinguished because the picture is so mixed. This again is a *Denkfehler*, because, as we have already pointed out in the case of the ruined cathedral, as long as any signs of order have escaped complete destruction in the general ruin, these "broken bits and pieces remaining of the flying buttresses and Gothic arches" will still show what sort of men planned them. Thus, even widely separated little pools of beauty, love, joy, order, healthy bodies and virtue which remain in the general hate, war, destruction, chaos and ugliness of the world of nature in which we live, still point unflinchingly to the Architect who designed and produced it before ruination set in.

In fact, as seen in the cathedral, when chaos replaces order, it can often lay bare and dissect the original order better than could the intact orderliness of an organism, or unruined nature itself. The study of cancer cells—a good example of the ruination to which living entities can easily come—has laid bare many secrets of the healthy intact cell which would never have been suspected had we had only normal healthy cells under our microscopes.

SUMMARY

Therefore, we can maintain that even though the creation around us is certainly a hodgepodge of good and bad, even though life certainly presents a badly mixed picture, it is still untenable to conclude with my professor that this means there is no Architect behind it, that everything arose due to chance and long timespans. Any little pool of love or order in the general rubble heap of nature must lead us to a mind or Designer behind that pool, no matter how small and smothered in rubble it may be. Thus, a synthesis is possible, and the teaching of Romans 1 that the universe reveals enough of its Maker to bring any logical person to his knees in thankfulness and worship is confirmed.

CHAPTER

4

The Origin of Evil

Difficulties of the type discussed in Chapter 2 led Baudelaire, the French art historian and poet, to exclaim, "If there is a God, He is the devil!" Such a statement is the direct result of believing that man has always been as he is, good and bad, and was so designed originally.[1] This is the Muslim position.

Theistic evolutionists cannot avoid the same difficulty when they maintain that God used evolutionary processes to produce the world of nature as we see it today. If He did, then His methods made the bad with the good, as Baudelaire maintains, and He therefore must be the devil as well as God. Everything pivots on whether we believe nature was once good and then subsequently ruined, whether we believe in the fall of man as laid down in Genesis. By tampering with the structural details of Genesis, we are likely to garble the whole reason for the present state of man—and the whole plan of his salvation which will take him out of the present disastrous mess. Genesis presents an integral whole on which the total plan of Scripture is firmly founded.

Let us return to the cathedral illustration of Chapter 3. It is superfluous to point out that all illustrations and analogies are imperfect and have their weaknesses if pressed too far. Our illustration of the cathedral is no exception. One of its imperfections lies in the fact that the architects who designed and built the cathedral are long-since dead and therefore could not prevent the bombing of their masterpiece. Then is God dead too? Was He dead when His masterpiece, nature, was bombed into ruin?

Today, many assume God to be, in fact, dead and resolve the question that way. But this is a doubtful escape exit for several reasons. Although it might explain God's creative work in the past and its subsequent ruination, it would never explain the present maintenance of nature and creation. No dead God could take care of that. Christians rightly believe that He is not only the living Creator, but also the living Maintainer of nature—and of us. By very definition, the "God is dead" theory will not fit in here, for maintenance implies activity and life.

Thus the question now becomes: Why didn't an almighty God who made, maintains and presumably loves His masterpiece, creation, prevent its bombing? Here the parable of the cathedral can do us no more service.

People who continually ask the question, "Why doesn't God stop it?" are often those who don't bother to ask what "stopping it" would entail. Some specific details must be examined before attempting to solve the greater principles involved.

Consider any virtue of which a person is capable; love, kindness, honesty, faithfulness, chastity, or any of the traits named in Galatians 5 will do. Select a virtue which pleases us all — love — and ask the following question: What is the nature of love in particular, and virtue in general?

NATURE OF LOVE AND VIRTUE

This subject of the nature of love and virtue is vitally important because the Christian way of life maintains that God Himself is love. Christians in the Western world often do not realize the tremendous import of this statement. I have given other religions, including *Islam*, some thought and have studied *Islam's* holy book, the *Koran*, which designates *Allah* as the compassionate, forgiving one. As far as I know, nowhere in the *Koran* does *Allah* figure specifically as an embodiment of love. He may threaten, may be merciful, omnipotent, compassionate and omnipresent. He may offer the faithful a place in the gardens of paradise with as many dark-eyed *houris* as they wish.[2] But love never figures in the *Koranic* revelations of *Allah's* nature. A designation of God as love stands unique in the Bible.

Right in the center, then, of the Christian position is this virtue we call love. It must be of vital importance for that very reason.

Nevertheless, I find myself at an extreme loss when I am asked to rationally explain anything at all about God's love. I know that "God so loved the world that He gave His only Son, that whoever believes in Him should not perish but have eternal life."[3] But God, even though loving, is also infinite. Therefore, He exceeds anything my thinking apparatus can handle. So I do not pretend to be able to plumb the depths of either His love or character. To think rationally about that love is far beyond me.

I suspect it is for this reason that when the Scriptures speak of God and His love, usually man's love to a woman and vice versa is used to drive home the point at an anthropomorphic level. It is like using real-life illustrations to clarify abstract and abstruse points of chemistry to non-scientific people. Thus, God provides information on Himself and His love in a human setting in order to really communicate with us. The information we thus obtain by "cutting down the high voltage of God's love" to the "low voltage of human love," we will then apply to our main problem.

The first question in analyzing human love is: How did this love between bride and bridegroom originate? The history of most such relationships provides the answer. The young man met the young girl one day and sooner or later began to feel attracted to her. The attraction is better experienced than described. Very often the girl feels attracted to him at the same time, although she might at this stage be more hesitant to display her feelings. Often he begins the action side of the relationship by looking for suitable ways to court her. But until wooing is begun, the whole affair is lopsided. A one-sided relationship in which attentions are not returned can be extremely painful. Certainly it is neither happy nor satisfying to either party.

At this stage there is one burning question which every prospective bridegroom would like answered as soon as possible: Does she love me? Is my attraction to her reciprocated? One purpose of courtship is to give the girl a chance to settle the question in her own mind. For once she notices the man's attentions and therefore, attraction towards her, she has to make a momentous decision: Can I return his affection? If she thinks that she may do so, then she must decide if she can love him. Here she must rely on her own heart, as well as on her common sense and the principles of life to which she adheres. After due consideration, she may decide she does. An understanding is reached between the two. A radiant couple emerges, and great are the happiness and joy of two hearts that have entrusted themselves to one another in mutual love and faithfulness.

In order to answer the question why a God of love just doesn't "stop it" we must analyze this process of falling in love more closely in order to draw some reason out of what often appears to be an entirely unreasonable happening.

First, the young man must court the girl of his choice. She will be unhappy if he doesn't and he will be unmanly if he doesn't know how! Now, courtship is a very fine art, besides being a very necessary one. Some of our finest poetry, music and art have arisen as its byproducts! Most important, perhaps, is that it is a so-called gentle art, which brings us to a cardinal point in our analysis.

The moment force takes the place of wooing, both love and the joy of love cease. They are often replaced by hate, recriminations and misery. For the whole structure of love is built on absolute mutual consent and respect for the character and sovereignty of the loved one. In other words, the structure on which human love between a bride and a bridegroom is squarely based is freedom to love.

Most civilized societies recognize precisely this structure in their marriage services. The two persons intending marriage are both given the public opportunity of making a free will consent in saying "I will" before the assembled congregation. Old Testament cultures stand for exactly the same principle, as the following well-known story emphasizes.

REBEKAH

When Eliezer, Abraham's servant, asked Rebekah to become Isaac's wife (Gen. 24), he became so assured that he had found God's choice for his master's son that he was ready to cut corners in the process of taking the bride home. The evidence that Rebekah was God's choice was so overwhelming that he wanted to speed things up, intending to take off immediately with the girl and forget about all the formalities or ceremonies.

However, Rebekah's relatives saw immediately that this was no basis for marriage, even though the Lord might be in it. What a good thing it would be if young couples saw this point too, instead of just starting to live together with no ado or ceremonies. It is to emphasize the necessity of mutual public consent before love and lifelong married joy, the greatest relationship in our earthly life, that Rebekah's relatives got together and said that even though God might be in it all, Rebekah must first be publicly questioned on the matter. She had to give her own decision and opinion before they would let her go to Isaac. So they called her in before the family and their friends to ask whether she wanted Isaac. Only after she had given public consent, based on her own free will decision, did they agree to marriage. They knew that no other basis was good enough, even though it was obviously God's will even without such public decision-making.

THE AMNON AND TAMAR AFFAIR

Thus, the first point arising out of this analysis of the basis of bride-bridegroom relationships and love is that such a partnership is based firmly on public mutual consent or free will.

The second point deals with the consequences of neglecting the above point. The shocking "love affair" between Amnon and Tamar (2 Sam. 13) illustrates this danger in a crass way. Amnon fell madly in love with the king's beautiful daughter Tamar. He was so infatuated with the fair girl that he just could not wait to woo her and win her consent. By guile, Amnon arranged to be alone with the girl. Feigning sickness, he received the king's permission for Tamar to come and cook for him in his apartment. Having got rid of everyone else, he proceeded to force the poor girl because he was so madly "in love" with her. Love that cannot wait to woo is abnormal. It often metamorphoses before our eyes into lust.

The consequence of this haste and trickery was that Amnon's love turned in a twinkling into hate for her. The eventual result was murder, for her relatives had Amnon murdered later for his brutality and treachery. Tamar suffered heartbreak and "remained desolate in her brother Absalom's house" (2 Sam. 13:20).

FREE CHOICE

In order to love in this sense—not merely physical union, which can result from lust—we must experience the mutual attraction and union of body, soul and spirit in an exclusive personal relationship.

If the basis of mutual consent in the love relationship is removed, if there is no freedom to love, if freedom is replaced by force, then all possibility of loving is removed. Love can be replaced then by its opposite—hate. This implies, of course, the further step of logic: where there is true freedom to love, there is also freedom not to love. If this freedom to say "no" were not really present, there would *ipso facto* be no freedom to say "yes" and to love. The ability to say "no" must be just as genuine as the ability to say "yes" if true mutual consent is to be achieved as a basis for love.

As we have seen, the Bible teaches that God Himself is love, and His love is often likened to the bride-bridegroom relationship. Our third conclusion is that, if His love to us is to be compared in some way with our human nuptial love, then the principles governing the two loves can be expected to be comparable in some ways. We should expect God on this basis to be the grand wooer. That being the case, we should expect Him to be awaiting our response to His wooing. To receive and experience His love we should expect the mutual-consent basis to decide everything—my consent to Him in answer to His attraction to and love for me.

Thus, we conclude that if God is love in this sense of the word, He will be looking for answering love from me. Love is only satisfied if it is returned. He woos us by many means, mainly by having sent His Son, the second Person of the Trinity, to justify us by dying and being resurrected for us.

Being love, we would not expect Him to demand or attempt to force love. That would be a contradiction. The very attempt to do so would destroy the basis of all love. As our true lover He does everything to show the true nature of His love—even to becoming a fellow man, heir to our lot as well as bearing our sin. Jesus was serious about His love—serious even to death.

THE CASE OF THE ROBOT

Consider one more vital point. What would have happened if God had so constructed man that he could not make a true free will decision himself but was only capable of automatically doing God's will, just as a lock opens when one turns the correct key in it? If man had been so constructed that when a certain button in his mind was depressed he delivered love automatically, would real love be in fact delivered? Of course the answer is negative. Such a person would be congenitally devoid of free will and therefore incapable of love and virtues in any real sense of the word.

None of us would be interested in loving the outward form of a partner who, every time we touched a certain button, put chocolate in its mouth or stroked its hair, automatically intoned the sentence, "I love you." If such a system were conceived or constructed, it would have to be subhuman or machine by nature. For to try to construct it so that it delivered virtue or love on command would of necessity mean that it be devoid of humanity, and therefore personality, and as a result it could deliver nothing of the kind. Assume that God, in order to be sure of our love and to make sure that we were virtuous in every way, made us like marionettes. He would have taken from us the possibility of really exercising our free will in order that we might not exercise it wrongly. Wanting to be so sure that we loved Him and our fellowmen, He would have made us so that we could not do otherwise. Whenever He pressed a button, we would deliver the goods, just like a vending machine. How could such a set-up involve real love in any way?

THE GRAND RISK

This brings us right up to the great principle. If God wanted creatures that really loved Him and their fellow-beings, then He was, by the very intrinsic nature of love, obliged to recognize the fact (though it sounds strange to us to use such phraseology and maintain that God was forced to do anything —His own moral nature brings with it the consequence that He will or must act according to that nature) that love and virtue demand absolute freedom to love and exercise freedom. Such a necessity lies in the very structure of love and, indeed, of any other true virtue. Thus to create the possibility of love, God had to create free personalities just like Himself, for He is love and He made us to love.

For God to plan at all for true love involved the built-in risk of the proposed free partner-in-love not loving at all. To have built the love-partner so that he would be congenitally obliged to respond would have been to destroy the whole purpose of designing a creation where love could reign. God wished—and still wishes—to set up a kingdom of love on earth and in heaven. But to do so involves the above-outlined risk of the free partners choosing not to love, but to do the opposite of their own free will—or even to hate. The practical result of being indifferent to or hating is the same from the divine partner's point of view. For there is no positive response to his love in either case. And love aims at a response of love. Thus, either love grows by responding, or it dies.

ALMSGIVING AND THE SOCIALIST STATE

Exactly the same risk is involved in planning any and every virtue. Take for example the virtue of almsgiving. In Turkey one sees hundreds of needy beggars. There are the blind holding certified photographs of their suffering wives and children needing support. There are those lying in the gutters with their misshapen bodies uncovered so that all who pass by can see they are not counterfeiting. There is the poor man who has his feet where his shoulder should be, loudly and slowly repeating selected passages from the *Koran*. There is the old man suffering from Parkinson's disease, whose saliva continually runs over his poor old dirty face as he holds out an empty trembling hand all day long. Seeing this misery causes one to exercise compassion and give a coin so that they can eat a slice of good Turkish bread. Naturally one is convinced that something much more fundamental should be done for these thousands of people so representative of suffering humanity. But a coin will at least guarantee that the immediate plague of gnawing hunger will be assuaged.

So one gives something to the poor mother sitting in rags underneath the mailbox at the post office with her week-old, unwashed baby on her ragged lap. In so doing one exercises a virtue — that of almsgiving. The immediate reward is an extra-fervent prayer to *Allah* for the giver's salvation. The joy on the recipient's face would be reward enough. To exercise any virtue is a free will operation which brings joy to the giver and to the receiver.

If, however, beggars are cared for by taxes and the city authorities send me a tax bill to help support the poor and needy, then I must pay. It may be a good thing to organize matters in this way. Many maintain that this method is less degrading for the poor and that the burden is more equally distributed. I agree with them in this respect. But let us be clear about one of the overlooked consequences.

In paying my taxes which are used to support the poor and the needy, I no longer exercise the virtue I did when I gave the alms to the poor young mother. I might have paid about ten dollars in taxes for the poor, or I might have given the young woman ten dollars to buy her baby something better than dirty rags. The sum of money involved is irrelevant. In one case I exercise the virtue of almsgiving (and reap a blessing) while in the other case I must pay my taxes, grumbling perhaps about the waste perpetrated by the bureaucracy of the tax office, with no consequent blessing, even though I may be perfectly right.

In one case I exercise no virtue. In the other case, where I give of my own free will in almsgiving I exercise a virtue — simply because I do not have to act. Therein lies the difference: forced charity is no charity — and forced love is no love. Love and virtue melt in the grip of force just as ice melts under the pressure of a vice.

If I force my children to be good when we are out visiting, they may be outwardly exemplary—sometimes they are! I am thankful for this, but I recognize the fact that most parents will be familiar with—that this goodness may not be even skin deep! Force itself, unaided, can make no one good and virtues tend to fade away in its presence.

These considerations disclose one of the fatal weaknesses of our increasingly socialized world. All charity and works of love tend to become organized by the state, which rightly wishes to eliminate the humiliation to which the poor are subjected in accepting certain kinds of charity. The joy and virtue of true charity and love disappear immediately when the forced tax replaces the free will offering. The Lord Jesus Christ Himself remarked that it was more blessed to give than to receive, thus emphasizing the blessedness or happiness accompanying the free act of giving.

The exercise of any real virtue ennobles and enriches the character, giving real joy and radiance to those practicing it. Thus the socialized state often robs its citizens of the flights of exuberance to which free exercisers of love and charity are heir.

GEORGE MULLER'S ORPHANAGES

Over a century ago in Bristol, England, George Muller set up his orphan homes which were run and staffed entirely by the free will offerings and services of Christians in sympathy with his aims. Witnesses of Muller's work said that these homes full of the victims of suffering were real havens of love, joy and rest to thousands of orphans. Today many such orphanages (not Muller's) have been taken over by the state. The state institute is often merely a matter of rates and taxes, and the person in charge is sometimes a career person who makes no attempt to be a mother or a father to the children. Often the atmosphere of such an institution is as cold and devoid of love as the concrete bricks of which it was constructed. Scientists have shown that children in such institutions die from lack of love as often as they die from disease.[4]

The welfare state, in taking over everything to remove a few real abuses, too often kills love and the other virtues which make up the atmosphere of a home. Removing the freedom of service, the voluntary basis, causes love to evaporate. Not only do the children or inmates of these institutions suffer. The ennobling of character which the voluntary staff members would themselves receive by free will service is lost by their becoming merely career people. The more the world loses this right to freely exercise true charity, the harder, colder and more bitter it must become.

This disastrous effect is seen in the character of most socialized nations. In fact, it is producing just what Hitler produced in Germany by the same means: de-personalization—people who may do their duty but who will not raise a finger to help close a concentration camp if it involves personal risk. Their characters have not experienced the ennobling, strengthening effect which results from the exercise of freedom. Hitler was a living example of a man naive enough to attempt to demand and command the love and affection of his people. He may have realized at the end that love evaporates under just such pressure. The strength of character necessary to withstand any tyrant is not likely to be built in any generation without the ennoblement of character resulting from long exercise of the various human virtues we have discussed. Such strength will also overcome the various vicissitudes of life which often complicate the career of anyone strong enough in will to be ready to suffer for his own conscience's sake.

The tendency today is to push everything onto the community, resulting in private character impoverishment. We all know the person who doesn't want to get involved. The second tendency, contingent partly on the first, is to bring up every child to conformity so that only the will of the community and majority counts. Thus the steel of a private conscience, independent of conformity to the mass, does not develop. In Hitler's Germany, this was seen at its extreme development. People saw corpses dropping out of vans coming from concentration camps as they passed through a big city. But fear had so eroded characters that no one did anything—it was too dangerous to get involved!

In Chicago a few years ago I was walking from the Chicago and Northwestern Railway Station as I saw a man in a car literally plow his way through a group of old ladies as they crossed the street on a pedestrian crossing with a green light. He knocked one old lady down, injuring her. I took the license number of the car, which did not stop, and asked for witnesses. Many young women and men going to work in a neighboring shoe factory had seen the incident. But all backed away, muttering something about not getting involved. I didn't get a single witness.

The idea of the community providing for everyone's need "from the cradle to the grave" may be excellent from a purely humanitarian point of view. But, insofar as it takes away personal initiative, the realization of the scheme will never provide sterling characters ready and willing to suffer for conscience's sake and to stand alone, if necessary.

THE CREATION, SEEN AND UNSEEN

The Bible reports that when God contemplated the creation of the worlds seen and unseen He wished to construct them so that they reflected His very own nature and character. To do this, He had to build on freedom of action. He is free, so He had to make man and angels free too. Man was made "in His image"—that is, as a free personality, just as God Himself is. For even "His service is perfect freedom" and therefore founded and maintained in love. Accordingly, the angels who serve Him, including their chief Lucifer, the light-bearer, were given natures capable of genuine love to their Creator and toward their fellows. They were capable of wooing His love and being wooed by Him so that the perfect joy of love could reign in that kingdom. But this very possibility had to include the option of rejection. They were no puppets.

The Bible reports, quite as a matter of fact, that a large proportion of the unseen host showed that it really was capable of the joy of that kingdom of love and—by a very real proof—of rejection! Therefore, Lucifer did in fact show that he could love, in that he began, for reasons of pride, to reject the one perfect Lover, his Creator. Turning his back on Him, who is the sole good, Lucifer became the epitome of the bad. So arose the cursed, loveless and hateful ones who in the exercise of their characters now turned away from the good toward the bad and proceeded to destroy the good creation. Men become devils by exactly the same process. Obviously God, His nature being love, did not immediately take away all freedom of action and choice from His creatures, thus removing the possibility of a return to love. He allowed them still further freedom of choice, which meant in their case still further destructive activities being permitted. If He had taken away this possibility of freedom of choice at the first sign of rejection of love, He would have destroyed any further possibility of a return to love. So He has given us all a long time of freedom of action, that is, freedom to love, so that the kingdom of love can still begin again to rule—if man and angels want it. To have stopped it all at once by the strong hand of dictatorship would automatically have destroyed the very purpose for which the Creator had created His universe—in order to set up a kingdom of love in the seen and the unseen.

Therefore, this very existence of evil in a world created by an almighty, but also a loving God actually illustrates that the good and the virtue in it are genuinely good. Love in such a kingdom really is love and not anything else. Sometimes it is taught that love is a covert form of egoism, etc. The state of our fallen world really shows this to be impossible—the love of God in a world of blood is genuine enough!

Destroyers and haters usually want company in their activities. So when the chief, Lucifer, the light-bearer, had become the destroyer and the hater, he immediately approached Eve to make her and her husband become a part of his company of destroyers. The pair was also capable of true love. They possessed true freedom of choice, as is shown by the actual choice they made. They too turned their backs on the good, automatically becoming polarized to the chronically bad. So the whole seen and unseen creation of love became a creation of the wrong choice—the choice which turned its back on the source of all ultimate good. In leaving open a chance for seen and unseen creation to return to the ultimate good, God did not stop the bad. The free choice was still left open, leaving ruination and its cause still intact. That is the reason why God allows it—to provide a genuine chance for the return of love in general.

THE DIGNITY OF MAN

But does not all this lead to one main conclusion? Does it not all go to show the truly high esteem in which God holds His creatures, man included? It means that God really takes our decisions, our thoughts and our selves seriously. He even goes to the lengths of wooing us to make our decisions ourselves. He does not so construct us that we are puppets who have all decisions programmed—even though many physical processes within the body are pre-programmed.[5] True love is, in this respect, always the same—it always esteems and respects its partner. It takes the partner seriously.

The same thought also expresses why God bothers to woo men by "the foolishness of preaching"[6] and not by sending, as He could, mighty angels with His message. Perhaps they would only succeed in terrifying poor humanity if they appeared in their supernal splendor. God's purpose is to win man's simple trust and confidence, to win our devotion and genuine love. Therefore, He uses the natural methods available to win our decision for Him. If He overawed us in any way, that might make craven slaves of us rather than wholehearted sons. If He were to browbeat us into submission, He would only gain what

Hitler did—the abject, groveling fear (if not secret hatred) of his would-be partners.

Thus a God of love avoids like the plague the dictator's methods in dealing with man, the object of His love, and uses the lover's better method. It is very fundamental to see that one cannot terrorize people into love. Consider the miracles Jesus performed in this light. He never used a show of divine power in healing to frighten people into belief. In most cases, after doing some mighty healing deed, He admonished those who had seen the deed or experienced it to keep very quiet about it. Jesus' warning "tell no man" is almost proverbial in this respect. The fact is, God does not wish to force our intelligence or our will to reduce us to the state of cringing slaves. He wants redeemed sons who of their own free will, love, respect and gladly serve Him.

THE DEGREE OF MAN'S FREEDOM

Thus we conclude that man must be free indeed if he is ever to be able to love indeed. There is a consequence to all this which the reader will have surely noted already. It is this: Is man so free that God has abrogated all authority over him? Can man do exactly and precisely as he likes as long as he likes so that he can be said to possess a totally unfettered freedom in all directions as far as he himself chooses? Need he never fear that his Creator will intervene—all in the interests of man's ability to love and exercise virtue?

Although the Bible teaches that man has a bonafide free will and can certainly say no to his Creator's will and plan (the very state of our poor world shows that this is de facto the case), yet it teaches too that there are limits to that freedom just as there are limits to God's wooing activities of man. These wooing limits, it will be remembered, were founded in God's counsel from His side and in time from man's side. In the first place, God in His inscrutability sets a time limit for His wooing of our free will. Thus it cannot be said that we have perfect free will to accept or reject His wooing at any time. Our free will interacts with His free will to woo us and if He chooses to stop the courting process, our free will can do precisely nothing about the new situation. Here it is no longer unfettered. Second, repeated rejection of the goodness of God's courting sears the psyche of man, rendering it less and less receptive. This too is a process we cannot alter; it is like the second law of thermodynamics at work in our inward man, and our free will cannot alter it.

The same principle applies throughout man's kingdom in its relationship to man's Creator. Man can say no to his Creator for a certain time by expressing free will. But this process of saying no of our own free will to God interacts with God's free will and may produce a no from His side. For us dependent creatures this is the same thing as judgment supervening after grace. We all can turn our backs on Him and run away from Him and His goodness—until we reach what may be looked upon as the end of our tether. The tether represents the change in God from grace to judgment. How long that may take in each individual case of God's dealings is unknown to His creatures. This state of affairs is well seen in the case of the apostle Paul on the Damascus road. Paul had enjoyed perfect unfettered free will to rebel against Christ and had done so very successfully, until even he reached the end of the tether God had allowed him. Then God intervened severely, blinded him, and reduced him to the dependence of a child in his helplessness. But even in a drastic intervention of this type, the judgment of God was mixed with great mercy and it led to Paul's seeing the grace of God in restricting his field of unfettered free will. But perhaps his free will in the strictest sense of the term was not touched. Perhaps his knowledge was increased.

If we do not recognize some definite limits to our freedom, we risk abrogating God's ultimate authority and indeed sovereignty. Yet these limits in no way alter the conclusions we have drawn about the vital nature of freedom if we are to be able to love — or to rebel. One reason for this fact is that we ourselves do not know where the limits we are talking about lie. Therefore we are, to all intents and purposes, unlimited in our freedom from our own perspective. From our own point of view we are free to act, wander, rebel or love as under-sovereigns within a small area of God's sovereign kingdom. It is just within this area of real unrestricted freedom that real love and virtue can and do rule in us. Outside these unseen limits are areas of judgment and no-freedom. But since they are unknown to us, they are for practical purposes fictitious for us and thus of no concern in our decisions to rebel or to love.

The very fact that man has never succeeded in devising a formal proof of God's existence shows how completely God can and does hide Himself and His limits from our eyes. This being the case, most men act within the area of their own lives as completely free agents as far as their intelligence is concerned. This makes their decisions in that frame of mind completely free will and therefore valid from the point of view of exercising true virtue. We conclude then that the limits God has set for all mankind do not alter our decisive free will and its accompanying power of love or rebellion. These very limits maintain God's sovereignty while allowing man free agency in the area of his own consciousness.

One more thing deserves mention at this point: the "tether" we have referred to as God's restricting hand on our free will should not be regarded as something fixed or static. It is not of a set permanent length. It is my belief that the more devoted a man is to God's will for him, the longer the tether will become. That is, the greater will be the radius of freedom of action. To stick to our analogy of a tether, we might say that its elasticity depends upon our will being congruent with His divine will. To use the words of the apostle Paul, to "win Christ" and to attain to His confidence in us is the same thing as saying that the more we attain to the width, depth and breadth of God's will, the more we attain to His sovereign freedom too. As one prayer book has it, "His service is perfect freedom."

CHAPTER

5

The Problem of Rebuilding

Just what would we expect a God of love to do after His creatures had chosen the wrong road — turning their backs on the only good?

The Scriptures say that even before the wrong choice had been taken either by man or angels, God, because He is omniscient, knew all about it. He had even drawn up careful plans in advance to cope with the situation that would arise, even though He was in no way responsible for it, nor did He cause it (cf Rev. 13:8; Eph. 1:4; Heb. 4:3; 1 Pet. 1:19-20).

This last fact—that God, if He is God, must obviously have been omniscient with respect to the fall long before it happened—has been a stumbling block to many. Actually, few real intellectual difficulties are involved in this matter if it is considered carefully.

If I observe a person carefully over a period of time, I may notice some of his little idiosyncrasies. He may say "Ah," for example, as a prelude to every difficult word he has to pronounce. Or he may twitch his eyebrows (or his ears) before relating a good joke. Gradually I learn to predict just what he is going to do before he actually does it. My previous observations allow me to do this with a fair amount of accuracy.

However, my ability to foretell his actions in no way makes me responsible for them when he acts. Similarly, the fact that God was able to foresee what Adam and Eve, the angels and mankind in general would do does not necessarily implicate Him in the sense that it makes Him responsible for initiating their actions and choices. The only implication is that involved in His having given them a gloriously free choice of action in order to create the possibility of their love.

THE PROBLEM OF THE CONSEQUENCES

At this point many will maintain that if God saw in advance the chaos, misery and suffering which would certainly follow the gift of the possibility of love, why did He proceed with His plans to create? Was He not rather sadistic to have persisted in these plans, knowing the consequences in advance?

In principle, the same type of questioning arises every day in our own lives, but seemingly we don't recognize this fact.

Consider for example the decision we must make on whether to marry. Even the marriage ceremony emphasizes rather drastically that the same question is involved, for the clergyman says our marriage vows are binding until death us do part. Surely there is scarcely greater grief than that experienced by a really devoted couple when separated by death. We could, of course, avoid this terrible grief by the simple expedient of not creating a marriage relationship at all! Avoid marriage and its love relationship and no grief of parting by death will ever overtake you.

Yet, we rightly go into marriage with our eyes open. We know that in normal circumstances death and all its sorrows will overtake us and will separate us. Most of us fear this more than we could ever say. In spite of all this we marry, because we believe that the joy of love and the ennoblement of giving ourselves to another in the abandon of devotion even for a day (and forty or fifty years pass like a day) is better than no love at all. It is written of Jesus Christ that He endured the sorrows of death on the cross for the sake of the joys which would result from the sorrow.[1] The same principle is involved here. The joy of love, even short love, because it stems from a God of love, compensates for even the sorrows of a cruel death such as that which Jesus suffered for all mankind, and the death which separates all lovers.

The enrichment and ennoblement of the human character brought about by the experience of even the brief joy of love, as God intended it to be, compensate for certain future death, separation and present trials. It is a question of balance. Those who know the love of God in Christ and those who have experienced a faint taste of that same quality of love in God-given marriage will confess that it is worth the certain severe suffering which it brings with it. The principle is that even a little, short-lived love is better than none at all. The reason is that even mortal love changes the eternal human psyche.

Evidently the Creator, being love personified, thinks this way too, for He did indeed create us and the rest of the fallen creation, in spite of the foreseen mess and separation.

All the same, many people—including ourselves sometimes—feel tempted to say "God, forgive, God"[2] when contemplating the dire mess in which the world finds itself. Yet, if it is true as the Scriptures assure us[3] that temporal sufferings can and do bring eternal recompense, if it is true that suffering is not necessarily punitive but can be remedial as well, then relying on the Scriptures we are able to accept the anguish just as God did when He crucified God to remedy the fall of man.

The next question is: What would we expect God to do to pull us out of the mire?

THE PROBLEM OF GOD'S ANSWER

Now that the fall has taken place and sin and anguish are in the world, what would we expect God's answer to be? The answer we give will depend entirely on our conception of God's character.

If God is a God of love, then He is our loved one. What would we expect a true loved one to do who had been misunderstood and rejected? Perhaps the scriptural answer is the best one

here: Love "suffereth long, and is kind ... is not easily provoked, thinketh no evil ... beareth all things ... endureth all
things ... (love) never faileth."[4]

Surely that is the reaction we would expect of someone who truly
loves us. Love endures all these things in the hope of ultimate
success in the wooing process of love. God saw man's wrong
choice and all of its consequences which would lead to chaos
and anguish long before the wrong choice was made. When it did
come, however, we would not expect a real God of love to impa-
tiently and disgustedly dismiss and destroy the object of His love.
Many who have difficulties with these points apparently expect
God to act like a hard-hearted, unforgiving tyrant rather than a
forgiving Father. Such an expectation probably arises from the
fact that such action is typical of short-fused people like ourselves.
But, then, we are no real examples of love in being short-fused.

In actual fact, we would expect a God of love to try to salvage what He could out of the carnage. It takes the patience
of genuine love to set about this process. He had warned in
faithfulness and sternness of the consequences of the wrong
choice—men would surely die of it—but neither angel nor man
heeded. One thing God would not be expected to do, once the
wrong choice had been taken, would be to block the way back
to Himself by attempting to threaten, cajole or force us back.
Force cannot restore anything in the way of love. That would
be to cut off all possibility of a way back.

HOW TO RESTORE LOVE

Thus, in order to restore love, there remains only one way
open—the exercise of further patient love. Accordingly, God

exercises long-suffering and patience in trying to win us back freely to love and reason.

Therefore, we should expect the consequences of the fall not to be fire and thunder, but rather the "still small voice" in the attempt to realize the word said about God by the apostle: "who desires all men ... to come to the knowledge of the truth."[5]

But this attitude of quietness and perseverance can be mistaken for passivity or even inactivity. A large part of the Scriptures is devoted to just this point, in fact. God is not inactive; He is not indifferent. He is certainly not dead: "The Lord is not slack concerning His promise, as some men count slackness; but He is longsuffering toward us, not willing that any should perish, but that all should come to repentance."[6] This means just what it says: not all men will repent and come to a knowledge of the truth. But it confirms that God is a God of love and patience who is ready and willing to receive all who do turn to Him.

The fact then that He has waited so long before judging sinful man is, in reality, another indication of God's true character—lovingkindness, patience, longsuffering, not being easily provoked. Only by looking at the situation in this way can I see any explanation of why God has not long since exercised general judgement on all of us and set up a "puppet state" on earth and in heaven to slavishly and immediately carry out His every demand, just as any dictator would do if he could, particularly if his will had been thwarted as God's will certainly has been.

THWARTING GOD'S WILL

Some will feel shocked. Can, then, God's will be thwarted? The fatalistic Muslims think not. Is it possible that His will may not be done on earth as it is in heaven? Anyone unsure about this point should ask himself whether God planned any act of sadism that has taken place. Was it His will to kill six or seven million Jews in gas chambers simply because they were Jews? Was this not, rather, thwarting God's perfect will? And does not any other sin also thwart it?

Sinning is one way of thwarting His will. Another way would be to set up a dictatorship to restore order to the chaotic creation. If this route to rebuilding creation were adopted, it would just as effectively thwart God's real purpose of setting up a kingdom of love. Under the present circumstances of freedom to do good or bad, there are still a few people who see the situation as it really is and who turn to God to be refreshed by His love, even in the midst of the general anguish of creation. Even a little of such love and refreshment is better than none at all. If the Lord had judged immediately after the fall or after any sin, how many who have since drunk of the water of the well of life and love would have been lost to Him and His kingdom of love forever? His patience has been rewarded with responding love, which would have been impossible if immediate judgment had supervened.

KING GEORGE VI OF ENGLAND

A story is told about King George VI of Great Britain and how he won Elizabeth. As a young man the future king fell in love with the charming young Scottish lady. After a long time of reflection he plucked up his courage and approached her on the subject, although he was rather shy, especially with the opposite sex. He had never been much of a lady's man and was neither very robust nor strongly masculine in the filmstar sense of the word. Moreover, he had a slight speech defect which added to his difficulties. His proposal was rejected.

The young prince, greatly upset over this rebuff, asked his mother, Queen Mary, for her advice. The Queen listened sympathetically to her son's tale of woe. Then she told him she just wanted to ask one question before advising him. Did he really love Elizabeth only? Would he be able to find a substitute if Elizabeth proved reluctant? After a moment's consideration, he replied that he would marry Elizabeth or no one else. "Well then," said his mother, "there is only one way open to you. Go and ask her again."

So the young prince put his pride in his pocket, gathered up his remaining courage, and arranged another interview with Elizabeth. He probably stuttered as he repeated his proposal, remembering what had happened to him the first time at her hands. She refused him again.

Not knowing what to do then, he returned to his mother, Queen Mary, for advice. Again she listened quietly—some say, severely—to the whole story. She showed him every sympathy and after hearing all he had to say indicated that she had one question to ask before she could advise him. The question was: "Do you really want her after this rebuff? There are plenty of other young ladies around who would be delighted to have a prince as a husband. I myself could show you some." But poor George was quite clear about his feelings. It was Elizabeth or no one at all. "Then," said his mother, "in that case there is only one way open to you. Go and ask her again."

So, after a considerable period of mental preparation, the young prince approached the pretty young Scottish lady the third time.

In the meantime, she had noticed how serious the prince was. His love and determination to win her had indeed been constant. She saw that the great effort he made in coming the third time, putting his pride in his pocket demonstrated his singleness of purpose. And she began to recognize something new in herself. His undoubted love toward her was beginning to kindle an answering fire in her own heart. His warmth of love, even though he was awkward and not very good at courting a young lady's affection, was beginning to warm her affection towards him. In short, his love was beginning to kindle her love, and she began to transmit some of the love she received from him. She began to feel she was able to say that she loved and admired him in his singleness of purpose and constancy. Thus, the story goes, began one of the really happy families in the annals of royal households. This love lasted until the king's death.

Love begets love. But it often has to be very patient, longsuffering and kind until the fire is kindled in the prospective partner's heart. The Scriptures say that God woos in one way or another every man and woman ever born.[7] Through the circumstances of life, or through the Scriptures, He quietly goes on as the years pass, until we begin to return to Him some of the warmth of love which He has for us. For we are told that God has His delight among the sons of men.[8] He loves us[9] indifferent or rejecters though we have been of His overtures towards us. He is working toward the day when we may begin to return to Him the same love, and to delight in His friendship as He will delight in ours.

Once kindled, this love must be regularly tended in order to maintain the warmth of the blaze which God intends our love to be—warming and refreshing to both partners so that both can rejoice in the happiness which love brings. God is love and we were so constructed in His image that we can only flourish when bathed in such love—breathing it in and giving it out.

But it would be one-sided to leave the story here. All love stories do not end this way. We must look at one other less pleasant possibility.

THE FINAL REFUSAL

There comes a time in every love affair where a final answer toward the wooer must be made. This final answer may be either yes or no. One day the wooed one may make a rejection which, although she perhaps did not know it, was the final one. It turns out to be permanent. In the one case, she may of course die. That finishes the wooing of a mortal man—when immortality lays hold of the prospective bride.

Another possibility is that the wooer may cease to woo. The wooed is not the only one who has a free will to accept or reject the wooer. God as the wooer has a free will too—to stop or to continue wooing according to His infinite wisdom. He can decide how long to woo and be rejected and also when to stop wooing altogether. Even this final decision to stop wooing will, we are told, be made on a basis of love. It will, accordingly, be put off as long as possible.

There is a third and last possibility. If the wooed marries another, then further courtship by the first suitor would be thoroughly out of order and outside the confines of love. The Scriptures say quite clearly that this state of affairs may be reached in the spiritual sense. There comes a time when a man "marries this world," and after that, God no longer offers His salvation, His marriage relationship to him. His Spirit strives with him no longer. A man's spirit and God's Spirit become forever estranged, for man's spirit finally "marries another," selling itself to this world and its rebellion against the Most High.

We humans can seldom clearly see when such a final act takes place. We cannot determine when God's Spirit gives a man up forever. But that such does occur is perfectly clear, even though it is invisible to man's mortal eye. We can give ourselves entirely over to material things such as a career, money or social standing. It may be the love of things more definitely sinful that cuts us off. In extreme cases, we can sell ourselves to the devil quite consciously — as many Nazis did when they knowingly cooperated with Hitler in liquidating human beings in the interests of their own promotion within the party. Many do the same just as effectively when they value promotion in their jobs before promotion in the kingdom of heaven. They do not seek "the kingdom of heaven first."[10] Some men resolve never to discuss spiritual matters again because "they disturb." For them, the courtship is over; they're married to another.

The New Testament letter to the Hebrews speaks of that cessation. "Today when you hear this voice, do not harden your hearts as in the rebellion, on the day of testing in the wilderness, where your fathers put Me to the test and saw My works for forty years. Therefore, I was provoked with that generation and said, 'They always go astray in their hearts; they have not known My ways.' As I swore in My wrath, 'They shall never enter My rest.'"[11]

The context of this statement shows that the Lord spoke and spoke again, and wooed and wooed again, but the Hebrews of that generation closed their hearts and inward ears. In the end God gave them up, and that generation, except for Joshua and Caleb, never entered the Promised Land but perished in the wilderness. This serves as a parable for us to whom God also speaks. We can be so occupied with the joys and trials of this life that we too do not hear. We too can miss the joy and rest of His love by acting as did the Hebrews.

"For it is impossible to restore again to repentance those who have once been enlightened, who have tasted the heavenly gift, and have become partakers of the Holy Spirit, and have tasted the goodness of the Word of God and the powers of the age to come, if they then commit apostasy, since they crucify the Son of God on their own account and hold Him up to contempt."[12]

This warning is to those who have at one time responded to God's wooing and have therefore tasted His goodness, and then cease to respond. A time comes when it is impossible to renew them, for the striving of God's Spirit with them ceases.

Another Scripture passage speaks in exactly the same tenor: "For if we sin deliberately after receiving the knowledge of the truth, there no longer remains a sacrifice for sins, but a fearful prospect of judgment, and a fiery fire which will consume the adversaries. How much worse punishment do you think will be deserved by the man who has spurned the Son of God and profaned the blood of the covenant by which He was sanctified, and outraged the Spirit of grace? It is a fearful thing to fall into the hands of the living God."[13]

I take this warning for myself, believing that I can learn from all Scripture. The point is, God can and does speak to men; He does woo. If they respond, He allows them to taste in this life the things of His kingdom of love. But His wooing is dynamic, and it is dependent on our daily response. Continual spurning may end in our "marrying another forever." Then His wooing stops. Rejecting God's grace in Christ simply means declaring ourselves as candidates for no grace, which is the same thing as being ripe for judgment.

This raises the whole question of judgment at the hands of a so-called loving and gracious God. Can we accept this? Is all suffering a judgment? Or must suffering and judgment be kept apart in our minds?

CHAPTER

6

Suffering: Is There Any Reasonable Interpretation?

RESENTMENT AGAINST PURPOSELESS SUFFERING

Many people as they undergo suffering resent what is happening because they can often see no constructive purpose behind it. Senseless suffering—such as we see when innocent children are destroyed or mutilated in war, sickness, plague or famine—makes our anger and impatience rise. The impatience increases when we see pain which is not only senseless or random but apparently designed and calculated, or even refined, as is the pain at the root of malaria.

A good example of apparent sadism arises in considering, as did C.S. Lewis, the deafness of a musical genius such as Beethoven.[1]

An absolute master of the art and science of sound struck down with stone deafness! Could a greater refinement of apparent sadism be conceived? Hence the impatience of many when they merely begin to consider the problem of suffering.

Yet, on the other hand, anyone considering himself to be a Christian is warned on every side to expect both joy and suffering as normally as summer and winter. Both are, according to the Scripture, integral parts of the Christian experience. Being a Christian does not provide exemption from suffering with the rest of mankind. Rather, there is the promise of additional suffering for Christians. The apostle Paul says explicitly that the Christian must enter the kingdom not only in joy but through the gates of many trials, tribulations and sufferings, being forsaken of man, and apparently by God too, before reaching the final gate of death.[2]

IF GOD IS GOOD, WILL HE HURT US?

Lewis puts this very question in another light when he writes: "If God's goodness is inconsistent with His hurting us, then either God is not good or there is no God; for, in the only life we know He hurts us beyond our worst fears and beyond all we can imagine."[3] Plainly, this means that if we believe in God at all, we must believe that it is consistent with His perfect nature, kindness and love to hurt us and to leave us wallowing in our own blood, as it were, right up to the end.

Lewis adds a rider to this statement which asks, in effect, if we accept that in this life God can hurt us beyond all that we can imagine, and that this hurting is consistent with His goodness, have we any valid reasons for believing that He should not, if necessary, continue hurting us in the same way after this mortal life is over?[4] Obviously there is no moral reason why He should not if spirits can endure suffering as mortal men do. Numerous passages of Scripture need to be examined carefully in this connection. Neither Lewis nor we are suggesting that the torments of hell are universal after death! The real question is whether suffering serves any purpose in this life and in that to come.

We can, however, go one step further and still remain on safe ground. If God has good reasons for hurting us now in this mortal life, He might conceivably have equally good reason for continuing the same process afterward in death. Clarity will only come by first asking ourselves, "What do the Scriptures say?" And second, from our answer to why He hurts us now, what He intends us to achieve by it in this life and beyond.

WAS CHRIST EVER IN MAN'S POSITION?

It is often helpful in dealing with such questions to find out whether Christ the Man was ever in the same position as we in regard to suffering. If He was, then the investigation of what suffering achieved in Him will perhaps provide the answer as to what it is supposed to achieve in us.

Accordingly, looking at one of the most obvious cases of Christ's suffering—the cross—may help to solve the problem. God the Father remained passive while millions of Jews, His own people, were gassed in brutal cynicism, just as He "stood passively by," as it were, while men crucified His own beloved Son.

To make matters worse, the Scriptures say that this brutal act was the culmination of the prophecy that Christ was the Lamb of God slain from the foundation of the world. Thus, the cruel cross was an eternally foreseen event—an event which God presided at eternally in an apparently passive manner in that He did not stop it. Therefore, the hurting of the Beloved One must have been consistent with God's eternal character. In fact, God Himself suffered, for He was in Christ as He suffered (2 Cor. 5:19), so God was actually not just passive during this event. He actively suffered.

THE CROSS AND GOD'S LOVE

This means that if the central doctrine of the Christian faith, the cross, is true, then it is obviously consistent with God's eternal love to hurt those He loves best, including Himself, even to the point of what we would call barbarism, for the cross is barbaric.

Whichever way we look we find the same picture in principle. Christ on the eternal cruel cross and a so-called God of love behind Him and, indeed, in Him. Humanity and biology for millennia "under the harrow" too, and yet allegedly according to the Scripture, a God of love behind us, who is until now entirely passive at the spectacle. Confronted with this situation, what Lewis feared was not so much a loss of belief in God at all with its concomitant victory of pure materialism in him. That solution would have been too easy, for it would have meant that a simple overdose of sleeping pills at any time could have gotten him out from "under the harrow" forever. Far too simple! What worried Lewis was that man and biology might be trapped as it were in a laboratory in which God might be the eternal vivisector and we the rats![5] Lewis says that the despair in which the Son of God died when He cried out, "My God, why hast Thou forsaken Me?"[6] might have been the result of Christ finding out that the cross was, in reality, a carefully baited laboratory trap which sprang at death and from which there was no escape after God had lured Him into it.

Looked at dispassionately, surely even a fallen person like myself, possessing scarcely a trace of the love I attribute to a God of love, could not have stood passively by while they crucified Him—or gassed millions of Jews. But then if we take that view, God must be morally inferior—even to me—which is completely nihilistic. We shall have to scrap that thought too, for it leads straight to the destruction of all rational thought on the subject.

Of course God is more compassionate than I. But then why was He so relentlessly passive at the cross? Why doesn't He relent at the millennia of human and biological agony?

HURTING IN ORDER TO HEAL

Might the key to the sore problem be found in the following considerations: Can we allow that to do good there are occasions when we must do that which looks as though it were bad? Put another way, can we hurt to heal? Obviously we can allow that, for every good surgeon and dentist does so regularly and routinely. If every time I flinched, gripped the dentist's chair, or drew back my head in pain at the relentless drill, the dentist were to stop and end the torture by filling up the still dirty cavity with amalgam, he would be less than a good dentist. He would not be being good, kind or loving to his patient if he were anything but absolutely unrelenting in his thoroughness in inflicting this therapeutic suffering. We would all be in trouble again in no time if he did relent. And then all the pain he had inflicted in earlier drillings would have been in vain. He has to be apparently passive to the pain he is causing. Does he seem devoid of feeling? In reality, of course, his passiveness to suffering, his apparent lack of feeling and his relentlessness are merely motivated by common sense and consideration for his patient, even though the intolerable pain might persuade me otherwise.

For anyone who has undergone a molar root treatment, two further points will emerge or throw light on this problem. The bacterial infection not only causes excruciating pain, but the toxins released into the blood will poison the patient to such an extent that his very consciousness may become clouded. He may scarcely know what he is doing because of the pain and poison. Then the dentist begins work with his awful drill. The pain becomes more excruciating until the center of infection is reached. Then the poison pressure is released, and immediate relief is felt, though it is not yet complete. As soon as no more poison is being released into the blood, the head begins to clear and the pain to subside.

First, then, in order to remove the hurt of decay, sometimes more pain has to be inflicted—worse than that of the original sickness. But the worst pain acts therapeutically on the first pain and purges it away. Second, only when the basic trouble begins to be cured does clarity of thought return.

THE SCRIPTURAL POSITION

Scripture teaches in essence precisely this view on the meaning of suffering. The fall introduced the decay of humanity and nature resulting in the hurt which afflicts us. To cure this festering mess, the Bible says a good but relentless Surgeon is needed to drill and drill until reality is too horrible to bear, until flesh and blood can no longer take it—until we believe we are forsaken by God and man. The Bible describes in detail both the setting in of the decay and its radical but painful cure. Our species has decayed from its original state and become, as it were, a lower or decayed species, as I have described elsewhere.[7] The cure requires radical and drastic treatment involving, first of all, the reaching of the focal point of the infection, and then the removal of the deformities caused by decay. Christ's death and resurrection reached the focal point of the trouble, as it were. But the deformities of the decay have also to be corrected, and that takes time and can be expected to be painful.

One of these deformities is connected with the clouding of the intellectual and rational processes which accompanies the fall. The apostle described them in Romans 1 as a "darkening of the mind" so that the normal logical thought processes for which we were designed become garbled. One of the byproducts of suffering is seen here. For although suffering and toxins may knock us silly, the removal of the latter can bring clarity of thought. It is a fact that sin darkens the mind. The corollary that redemption and holiness enlighten the mind is also true. For salvation not only redeems us from a lost eternity; it also redeems us from a lost, clouded, befuddled consciousness at present. By taking away our sin, we become saved for eternity. But we must not forget that this same saving process brings light and radiance to the heart and the intellect right now, the process being one of growth—growth in this life.

ACCURATE SURGERY OR WHOLESALE BUTCHERY?

Can the skilled, accurately aimed work of the dentist on a tooth with its concomitant pain and healing be compared with the wild, undisciplined, purely destructive agony which afflicts much of mankind today? Here again, for any satisfactory answer, we must turn back to the archetype of all barbarous suffering, namely, the cruel cross.

Is it possible to believe that when wicked men inspired by hatred and jealousy decided to take Jesus, hold a mock trial, scourge Him, display Him all night for the raucous amusement of the troops, and then finally drive iron stakes through His hands and feet, raising Him on a cross to bleed and suffocate to death—can we reasonably hold that such a performance was the work of a skilled Surgeon in His efforts to cure the world of its disease?

THE EXACT THERAPY OF THE CROSS

The Christian position is frankly that this was the case: that God, with the butchery of the cross, did cure the world of its disease; that the cross was the work of a skilled Surgeon, even though it looked from the human point of view like the exclusively destructive and adventitious work of the ribald Roman soldiers and hateful Pharisees. It looks so very much like this that the cross was considered by the Greeks to be so unworthy of Divinity that it was a sheer scandal. But the fact is, outward appearances may deceive.

The reason for this deception is simple. Outwardly wicked men put Him to death and that was all that man ever saw of the process. But behind the scenes the great Surgeon did an unseen work through Christ's suffering. Christ took into His own body the very virus which was at the root of man's sickness—the turning of man's back upon the only good One and His perfect will. The Bible says that this turning is sin. It is as though Christ in His death took the organism of decay (sin) away from me, as well as the toxic products of decay (sins) and allowed the organism to be cultured in His body until it killed Him. A parasite may kill the host organism, as when the influenza virus kills the man it lives on as a parasite. But in killing the host it also kills itself at the same time. So Christ took on the causative organism (sin) together with its toxins (sins) so that mankind could be freed from both by embracing His act.

This was the secret surgery or therapy which went on unseen to the human eye when they crucified Him. Thus, the senselessness of the cross is only superficial—superficial to the uninitiated. Its senselessness becomes sense to those who probe to the bottom of the mystery and find that He did, in fact, bear their sin and sins in His own body on the tree.

Christ at Calvary reversed the process of rejecting God's known will by turning to, embracing, and doing God's known will, even though it meant His own suffering and death. Man's act in turning away from God was reversed by Christ when He embraced God for us anew with His will. However, He embraced not only the basic cause of the ill—the turning away—but He took on Himself the consequences, the metabolic products as it were of that fatal wrong choice. He took my sickness and my sicknesses on Himself. No one knows just how He accomplished this, just what mechanism He used. All we know is that we could not do it, for none of us could die in a valid way before God for the sin of another. The Father gave His permission and command to Christ to lay down His life as a ransom for many. And Christ obediently did just that. The Man Christ reversed man's disobedience.

The Scriptures teach one other point on the meaning of suffering. Hebrews 5:8 teaches that even the Son of God learned obedience by the things He suffered. If the suffering of the dreadful cross produced positive results in the Son of God in this way, perhaps we are justified in thinking that even dreadful butchery of this Son may not be entirely negative in its effects even in our own case.

A LESS UGLY WAY?

This is, I suppose, the legal way of looking at the therapy Christ accomplished for me at the cross. As such, it is of vast importance, providing, as it does, the basis of salvation from the guilt of sin for eternity. Some will say it is horrible. It is. To think that God could find no other method than a bloody cross, cruel iron nails through His hands and feet, before He could redeem me from Adam's fatal mistake, fills me with dismay. Surely a more genteel, aesthetically acceptable method could have been found for such a momentous piece of therapy.

This brings us to the second point we must make on this subject. It concerns the blood, the sweat and the desolation of the cross of Calvary, in short, the ugliness and horror of such a piece of restorative therapy. The utter cruelty of it shocks even wicked men. Let us look, then, at this second great problem of the cross—its ugliness.

It is written of Christ: "In the days of His flesh, Jesus offered up prayers and supplications, with loud cries and tears, to Him who was able to save Him from death, and He was heard for His godly fear. Although He was a son, He learned obedience through what He suffered; and being made perfect He became the source of eternal salvation to all who obey Him."[7]

This is an almost incredible statement for the writer of the letter to the Hebrews to have made. The Son of God had always been perfect from eternity until He came into time at the incarnation. During the incarnation He was without sin and therefore still perfect. What the writer is teaching here will answer our question as to why God chose such a cruel method of redemptive therapy.

MADE PERFECT

The process of "being made perfect" referred to here means in this context being made mature. If a child is perfect in mind and body, there is nothing we can complain about. But his perfection as a child needs to grow into the mature perfection of an adult. This process is one of growth in body, mind and experience. There is no quick way around it. To be genuine, it must be gone through experimentally.

This is exactly what Christ went through as a man. He was perfect from a child onward. But the Bible says He grew in wisdom and stature—that is, He matured by His experience as a man. Even though He was the second Person of the Trinity, He was perfected by growing up as a man, for He gathered actual experience of manhood which He lacked experimentally before the incarnation. He certainly knew all about manhood before He became a man, because He was omniscient. But now He experienced manhood in the body—and matured or became experienced and therefore perfected in it.

Now notice what some of this manhood experience involved for Christ—something He as God had not experienced as a man before: "In the days of His flesh, Jesus offered up prayers and supplications, with loud cries and tears, to Him who was able to save Him from death." It was the fight between the will to be obedient and the terrible reality of a bloody death on the tree. Here we have anxiety, anguish and suffering—right up to bloody sweat—in anticipation of the abyss of such a death. He matured as a man by the experience of anguished prayer in faith to Him who could deliver Him. We are assured that He was heard because of His godly fear. But He was only saved from death by going down through death and thus being led out of it after tasting it.

The result then of this seemingly unreasonable and cruel death of the cross and the death which preceded it was that although He was a Son, yet He learned obedience through what He suffered. Of course, He had always been obedient to the Father's will—the two wills were always congruent and the Father loved the Son and the Son the Father. But here was a new experience of the anguish of facing death such as all creatures, but not God, face. The God of life was to die for all His creatures and share all their ugly experiences.

This anguish and suffering of the cross and the preceding events demonstrated that Christ was perfectly obedient to the Father in all things. The experience of the unnameable pain, anguish and despair of the cross did something to the incarnate Son of God which would have been impossible before the incarnation. The discipline, the setting of His face as a flint to go to Jerusalem to face it all, the refusal of even the analgesic (the myrrh) before the nails were driven through Him, all that perfected even Him, the Son of God — as Man. Thus, the fact of the cross laid down the legal basis for our salvation, but the bloody cross showed what suffering and anguish can do if accepted as Jesus accepted them. His death was expiatory for sin. But the manner of His death served at the same time as a teacher of obedience to God the Man; it was a maturer, a perfecter of the perfect One. If the Son of God as man was matured in His experience and learned obedience by it, then we find yet another secret, hidden element in the mode of therapy God introduced by His Son to cure the creation of its fatal malady.

It will be obvious then that purely legally, Christ's bare death — by any method — would have secured our salvation for eternity. However it was perhaps, not immediately obvious why such a shocking and barbarous route to death needed to be taken — a route which made the cross a scandal to the Greeks and a stumbling block to the Jews. No wonder so few of the Greeks or Jews could understand it without the extra information given on the subject of suffering by the New Testament — and by experience too.

SUFFERING-NOT SENSELESS

Thus, the anguish and suffering of the cross are not senseless. They are refined, even though drastic, therapy, hidden to the eyes of the mortal man in general. But their function teaches us why the whole Bible is full of references to pain, suffering and anguish. Every person who embraces the death of Christ (and His resurrection) as his basis for eternal salvation is warned to expect as a matter of routine sufferings of some sort. Christ having suffered in the flesh, he is told, is warning us to arm ourselves with the same mind—that is, to be on the lookout for the squalls of suffering which certainly await the consistent Christian.[8] In giving us salvation, Christ suffered. In accepting that salvation, suffering will certainly find us out.

Further, we are told that the disciple is not above his Master even in these matters.[9] This means that in this context if the perfection or maturation of the Master could not be effected without the anguish of suffering, neither can the maturation or perfection of the disciple be accomplished by any other means. The Christian who thinks he can get through without this sort of perfecting is living in a fool's paradise. The disciple is not above his Master even in learning matters.

The New Testament is full of teaching of this kind, teaching which is seldom even touched upon today, for by its very nature it is unpopular to the natural human. Paul the apostle, when writing to the Philippians, informed them that, "It has been granted to you that for the sake of Christ you should not only believe in Him but also suffer for His sake."[10] Surely it would have been unnecessary for Paul to have told the Philippians that it had been granted them not only to believe but also to suffer if just believing without suffering was an ideal state. Clearly, no one wants suffering. But, in the light of the above it must be a special privilege. Christ did not relish it. He sweated blood in anticipation of it. Yet He endured it as a privilege in view of the glory of the maturity gained by it.

This means, again, that even for us mortals senseless suffering need not be pointless. It may be more than the mere adventitious agony produced in a mortal body of flesh and blood. It can be the gateway to special results in our characters. In any case, it is poor policy to avoid suffering by disobedience, for Christ embraced trials and suffered because of obedience. It is the Christian path to try to follow the same policy. For by doing so Christ has been matured and exalted by the Father to His right hand. The Father has committed the entire government of the world into Christ's capable hands—hands rendered mature and fit for the job by being obedient even to letting them be pierced at the cross.

Is it because the fruit of suffering is so little known in the Western churches that we have so few giants in the land today?

In the East the total number of Christians has been reduced greatly by suffering. But the proportion of giants, mature Christians, has certainly increased there.

PROMISED TRIBULATION

The Bible—both the Old and the New Testament—is crammed with references to suffering, anguish, tribulation, grief, trial and affliction.[11] For example, there is this rather neglected text by the apostle Paul: "But whatever gain I had, I counted a loss for the sake of Christ. Indeed I count everything as loss because of the surpassing worth of knowing Christ Jesus my Lord. For His sake I have suffered the loss of all things, and count them as refuse, in order that I may gain Christ and be found in Him, not having a righteousness of my own, based on law, but that which is through faith in Christ: that I may know Him and the power of His resurrection, and may share His sufferings, becoming like Him in His death, that if possible I may attain the resurrection (out) from (among) the dead."[12]

THE REASON WHY

It is clear from the letter to the Romans that Paul knew and experienced salvation on the basis of a gift of God and not on the basis of any works he had done. Nothing he could do could save him from the penalty of sin. On the Damascus road he had learned that his own works could not help him but that Christ's work could and did. Why then does Paul now insist so much on the value of the work of suffering he had done in losing everything for Christ's sake? Those losses would never save him.

As we read the cited passage carefully it becomes obvious that Paul is referring to the value of suffering and losses in learning the surpassing worth of knowing Christ. He is referring to a process which can only be described as one of Christian maturity or perfection. He suffered the loss of every privilege which he had possessed as a well-respected Pharisee in order to be obedient to Christ. No doubt this caused anguish. But his losses were not only abstract. He was whipped, imprisoned, mishandled, shipwrecked and generally maltreated as he went off scouring the world for Christ's sake. He couples these experiences with the greater experience which resulted directly from knowing the surpassing worth of Christ. Most of us Western Christians know little of this. Is it because we have not sought out the only maturing process known in Scripture leading to this knowledge—and to Christ? Paul's obedience, like Christ's obedience, in suffering while doing the will and Word of God is the key to such depth of experience.

But more about the maturing process is to be discovered in Philippians 3. Christ was exalted to power because He was fitted for it by the things He obediently suffered. Paul says in effect precisely the same of himself and his own exaltation. For he couples his loss and his suffering with a capacity to take part in what he calls the "out-resurrection" (*exanastasis*) which he regarded not as a matter of course for every Christian but as that which depends on Christian maturity. We all know—as do the Muslims—that all of us, small and great, wicked and good, rich and poor, will be resurrected at the great day of final judgement to receive the things done in our bodies. But before the day of general *anastasis* there will be an *exanastasis* of rising of the dead, not in general, but in a special resurrection. This will be at the time of the return of our Lord in glory to set up His kingdom on earth and reign. Christ is looking for men and women among His redeemed who have allowed themselves to be matured for this high office—by means of the same process by which He was made fit for it—by anguish and suffering.

Apparently Paul's aim was to accept the same type of loss and suffering that his Master had gone through in order to become prepared himself for high office with Christ. All this is based on the free gift of salvation by the blood of Christ. But in building upon this sure basis of free salvation, a maturing or a perfection process occurs by means of suffering in the will of God, foreseen both by Christ and by Paul. Paul's attitude of heart is confirmed by his instruction to Timothy: "If we have died with Him we shall also live with Him; if we endure, we shall also reign with Him; if we deny Him, He also will deny us."[13] This surely clinches the matter. The Christian owes his redemption to the free gift of God. But he owes his degree of exaltation to close knowledge of the surpassing worth of Christ and close association with Him and His purposes in His kingdom, and to the maturation processes which fitted even the Son for His supreme office in the kingdom. The experiences of suffering, endurance and anguish in obedience to the will of God, no matter how outwardly senseless and adventitious they may appear, are the therapeutic instruments God used on His Son and uses on all His redeemed who declare themselves willing for the process.

The same process produces not only the surpassing knowledge of His will, but it also makes us useful to others. "For because He has Himself been tempted and has suffered, He is able to help those who are tempted."[14] On this basis, who could be better fitted to help mankind than the Son of Man who has been through the same kind of temptation—though far more acute? This establishes a bond of confidence between us and Him. He understands because He has experienced the fire of anguish. Therefore He can help us. Our lot and His as mortals were once congruous. It gives me confidence towards Him. If I suffer, I can help those who are suffering, even as Christ has helped me.

PERFECTION

This leads us to the third point. The first point was that Christ died and rose again to justify and redeem us, giving us the basis for fellowship with the holy God. The second point was that His sufferings and endurance were the means of qualification and maturation for His exaltation to the right hand of God the Father. In a parallel manner, the sufferings of Christians are calculated to mature them for high office in His kingdom. The third point is also directly concerned with suffering and its consequences. Peter develops the subject in saying: "Since therefore Christ suffered in the flesh, arm yourselves with the same thought (mind or will), for whoever has suffered in the flesh has ceased from sin, so as to live the rest of the time in the flesh no longer by human passions but by the will of God."[15]

Peter was referring to "suffering in the flesh," which he says leads to ceasing from sin in the flesh. But the same principle also applies to matters not directly concerned with the flesh, as he also confirms: "For one is approved if, mindful of God, he endures pain while suffering unjustly."[16]

This simply means that any discomfort we have to endure because of our faithfulness to God will eventually lead to our being "approved." In fact, Peter says that as Christ suffered the same kind of discomfort for our sakes, so He left us "an example, that you should follow in His steps."[17] This then is the line of action to which we "have been called."

Therefore, according to Peter, suffering leads to ceasing from sin and approval from God. Is it then any wonder that after His death and resurrection Christ asked the disciples questions that bring the whole problem of suffering into focus? Was it not necessary that Christ should suffer these things and enter into His glory?[18] The Christ should suffer and on the third day arise from the dead.[19] The same topic was the subject of Paul's three-week long argument with the Jews in Thessalonica: "And Paul went in, as was his custom, and for three weeks he argued with them from the Scriptures, explaining and proving that it was necessary for the Christ to suffer and to rise from the dead."[20]

AMONG OTHER THINGS, SUFFERING MADE CHRIST "APPROVED"

It is generally conceded that Christ's death is basic to the Christian's salvation. But the suffering type of death is not usually emphasized. Perhaps it is too barbaric for our cultured society to bear. Regardless of our reactions to the awfulness of death on the cross, God chose it in order to bring to mankind a full salvation—not only from the guilt of sin but also from its power, not only to save us from eternal damnation but also to demonstrate to us how to become approved in the same way that Christ became approved. In fact, it was to teach us how to cease from sin.

REJOICING IN SUFFERING

Paul sums it all up: "So we do not lose heart. Though our outer nature is wasting away, our inner nature is being renewed every day. For this slight momentary affliction is preparing for us an eternal weight of glory beyond all comparison."[21] Clearly Christ's death and resurrection are the cornerstones of any salvation that will take us to heaven. But Paul is talking about something built on the foundation of salvation as a superstructure. It is an eternal, incomparable weight of glory founded

upon salvation, God's free gift. And it is our suffering, borne
in the will of God, which makes us approved for incomparable glory, just as afflictions and suffering brought approval to
Christ after He had patiently and triumphantly borne them.
Temporary afflictions exchanged for an incomparable weight
of glory! Paul considered it a bargain. So he acted upon it
immediately!

A POSSIBLE MISUNDERSTANDING

Of course, one might say that if suffering is so useful and well
rewarded in the will of God, then let us afflict and scourge our
fellowmen all we can and seek suffering ourselves. We are doing
them a favor by hurting them or ourselves. This seems to echo
the old argument: let us sin willfully so that grace may abound.
Let us seek and provoke suffering! God forbid! The dentist does
not willfully or wantonly bore holes anywhere and everywhere
in our teeth to stop the future possibility of decay. God is the
Surgeon, so let Him operate just where it is necessary. He may
and will use wicked men as His scalpel. He has promised to pun-
ish them for their evil intentions because they afflict others just
for the sake of hurting and killing. Though He uses the same evil for
His purposes, that doesn't give us the right to sin so that grace
may abound by hurting others or ourselves unnecessarily.

To indiscriminately inflict pain is wanton. Jesus never regarded
pain and suffering as good things in themselves, for He abolished them by healing on many occasions. He also told us to do
the same. The Scripture speaks of death itself as the last enemy.
Pain falls into the same category. Pain and death entered into
the world by the fall, when man turned his back upon God.
The point is that God reverses the evils of pain and death to

produce a glorious result—to glorify His Son and to glorify man when they both withstand and endure pain and death in doing His will. This is how God triumphs over evil—not by stopping it, but by using it to His greater glory.

GENTLING PROCESS

A minister wrote to me on the subject of the meekness of Jesus, pointing out that the word "meek" is often misunderstood. In the context used in the Sermon on the Mount the word translated by "meek" really means "gentled" or "broken in" as those terms are applied to horses trained to work in a harness. The minister recounted how as a boy he had worked on a farm and helped with gentling horses, breaking them in for farm work. Later the horses were often used for pulling out tree stumps prior to preparing wasteland for arable purposes.

The untamed wild horses were useless for doing the skilled work necessary for removing tree stumps. They had to be thoroughly tamed before they could work constructively with other horses in teams. The taming or gentling process was a prerequisite for useful work. Once they had been submitted to the sometimes harsh process of breaking in, which involved punishment as well as rewards, they worked productively for the rest of their lives and obviously enjoyed it thoroughly. As their experience grew, the reins could be left on their necks and they would go by themselves from tree stump to tree stump, assume the correct position, wait for the chains to be hitched to the trunk, and then with all their strength—nipping and nudging one another in the process—pull out the stump. If a stump did not come up at the first pull they would move to a more favorable angle and try again.

Affliction and suffering can work as a gentling process, fitting us for God's work in the present world and the next. This is the true meaning of the word "meek" as Jesus used it. What if the abysmal suffering of mankind and of nature is now being used in God's good hands to gentle us all—even as it gentled His Son? The stakes are high indeed. Suffering makes us kind to others who suffer. But what if a bloody war, a rule of tyranny is really working out an incomparable weight of glory for all those who allow themselves to be gentled and disciplined thereby? If this is so, it would be a fatal blow for the despair and nihilism into which our generation is so obviously falling. If eternal glory were to result (and the Bible says it will), then we could, with the Christians of old, rejoice in suffering and jubilate with the apostle Paul: "We rejoice in our sufferings, knowing that suffering produces endurance, and endurance produces character, and character produces hope, and hope does not disappoint us, because God's love has been poured into our hearts."[22]

AGAIN, WHY ALL THE BARBARISM AND CRUELTY?

Some time ago I had the pleasure of discussing this and related questions with a U.S. Air Force chaplain. We came to two main conclusions which, as we shall see, throw light on the above problem:

1. We all have some sort of freedom to choose among the paths in life which are made available to us. But we never have any freedom of choice as to the consequences of any path we choose. For these consequences are the built-in properties of the way which we may freely have chosen. For example, though I choose the way of cheating in examinations, I cannot choose the consequences of

cheating. They are built into the way known as cheating. Similarly, I may freely choose to abuse drugs — it's entirely my own choice. But having chosen this way, I cannot choose the consequences of drug abuse such as drug dependence, liver necrosis, delirium tremens or hallucinations. They may be built into the path of drug abuse. The choice of the way is free, but not its consequences.

Man chose and still chooses to turn his back on the only good — God. Before doing this he was automatically part of paradise, for paradise was everywhere that God was. Having chosen good (God), paradise could not be chosen — it was part of the way with God, paradise was built in it. Of course, paradise included eternal and abundant life. However, later, in turning his back on God, man refused the way of paradise and chose the alternative way built into the choice of following Satan. The built-in consequences included such matters as pain, sorrow and death. Thus man found that after making his perfectly free choice for Satan, he automatically began to reap the consequences of this choice.

What can be done about the situation? To get man out from "under the harrow," to "pull the tines" out of his flesh now that they are there is painful too. Piercing flesh hurts in the first place, but so does pulling out the tines.

2. Suffering is not necessarily a judgment. Christ has assured us on that point.[23] In a way, suffering was a judgment — the judgment following a wrong choice. But curing the consequences of the fall is painful too. When we suffer, the pain may be either punitive or curative. It may also be a mixture of the two. Until we get behind the scenes of the material life, we

shall probably never be able to sort out the two. Nevertheless, both kinds of agony can serve to heal us.

IMPORTANCE OF THE STAKES

There is just one more point to be made in dealing with our problem. Probably few of us know what we really believe until we are asked to suffer some inconvenience or even pain for it. How much are we willing to suffer for what we really believe? The length we go along that road shows the depth of our belief. The Bible holds up Christ as an example—He suffered unto death because He totally believed in redeeming us. Some, like Falstaff, run away to fight another day, believing that discretion is the better part of valor. Surely such persons have shallow faith in what they fight for!

Christ loved His own, right up to the cruel death on the cross. This fact establishes forever His absolute faith in His calling to redeem the world. Second, it establishes the degree of His love toward those whom He purposes to redeem.

Therefore, it is obvious that suffering may act as a sieve or a filter to sift out the lighter elements of love and faith and separate them from the deeper ones. Suffering may show us what we really do believe as compared to what are only words and hot air. The little suffering that I personally have experienced has certainly shown me the shallowness of my faith in many directions. It produces a clarity of thought in these matters which is vital, for it leads me to repentance at the sight of my own shallowness in eternal matters. Therefore, suffering can act as the filter I personally need to sort out the wheat from the chaff in my own dealings with God, the good One. Fire must separate the dross from the gold in normal refining processes. But after enduring the fire, the gold is pure gold, though it may be less in volume than before the fiery refining process. Similarly, strong winds blow away the chaff and leave the corn.

THE JOY OF RELIEF

In C.S. Lewis' famous *Screwtape Letters* the "Law of Undulation" is used to describe the ups and downs to which all humans are subject. If we experience heights of joy, we shall also experience depths of misery. This is a perfectly normal process to which all flesh is heir.

This idea may be applied to our interpretation of the suffering of mankind. The person who has experienced the horrors of great pain is the most thankful, positively grateful, for any periods in which he experiences less or no pain. Such joy is unknown to the man who has not experienced pain.

The apostle John in the Revelation speaks of this type of exultation when he describes the arrival in heaven of those "who came out of great tribulation."[24] By the very contrast, that which they had suffered made their joy the greater.

It may be legitimately asked why the fall of man should have of necessity brought the suffering and death of which the Bible speaks. One can understand it having brought suffering and death to Adam. But why to the rest of the world? It does not help much to maintain that Adam was the head of visible creation which fell and that it fell with him. The creation under Adam was not rational as was Adam and therefore could not possibly bear the guilt that he, being rational, had to bear.

Our answer to this question really depends on our conception of the state of nature before the fall of Adam. When the Bible maintains that death and decay did not exist before Adam's fall, it is really introducing a concept entirely beyond the power of mortal man today to conceive of. For the idea of no death and decay cuts clean across our total experience of the laws of thermodynamics, particularly the second law. It implies no ageing—no entropy increase. The second law states that although the total energy in the cosmos remains constant, the amount of energy available to do useful work in the cosmos is always getting smaller with the passage of time. As I have pointed out elsewhere, this again brings with it the concept that chaos, disorder and decay are always on the increase with the passage of time in our total cosmos.[25]

Illness, decay, suffering and death can be regarded as accompanying symptoms of entropy increase. In fact, we measure the passage of time itself, in the last analysis, by the rate of entropy increase—how fast a clock, atomic or otherwise, runs down. The corollary holds equally well that without time there could be no increase in entropy. The same meaning conveyed by time-lessness and "no entropy increase" could be communicated by saying that an eternal or changeless state had been reached.

The creation of Adam, as described in Genesis, corresponds roughly to this external state of affairs. For we are introduced to him in Genesis not as a growing baby or as a maturing young man but as an ageless person. Even Eve, produced from Adam's flesh, was apparently ageless too—she was, at least, no infant when she appeared to Adam. In their innocent state there is no record of their having children, although Eve certainly had the sexual organs of a woman and Adam had those of a man. If they lived in a pre-fall world where no decay, no death and no second law of thermodynamics ruled, then reproduction there was not necessary—and, indeed, would probably have been an anachronism.

A consequence of all this is that a species living in a world in which the second law did not exist must have been vastly different from what we would expect today where the second law reigns supreme. For example, Adam before the fall could walk and talk freely with the Eternal, whose infinite dimensions he experienced as a matter of course. Traces of this ability are still seen in Moses and some of the prophets who moved in the eternal realm much more easily than we do. Christ did too.

If these considerations concerning Adam's state before his fall are correct, then everything in that primeval state must have been permanent or eternal—without time, entropy increase or decay, as they are in heaven or paradise. If the fall took place in such conditions of eternity and these eternal conditions had remained after the fall, this would have meant that the fall and its consequences are eternal too, and therefore irreversible. Adam would have turned his back eternally upon God and good, and his chances of returning would have been ruined forever. This is probably the state of the lost angels and Satan, who, living in eternity where no change in time can be, are lost forever.

Presumably then for this reason God threw Adam and Eve, and the creation over which they had been set, out of eternity—and its permanence in paradise—into time with its decay, sorrow and death. God introduced the second law, the law of impermanence and death as a measure to counteract the freezing of Adam's fall. So He rendered Adam's kingdom and its sin subject to time, the passage of thus providing a way back into the kingdom of love for which He had created man.

Death and decay became fully developed as a means of return when Christ used death to overcome the fall on the cross. This made the second law and its accompanying culmination in death the grand highway back from the fall to the kingdom, thus confirming what we have said above about its significance. Of course, the introduction of death and decay to biology introduced the necessity of reproduction, which did not exist in the realm of the eternal—just as it does not exist in the realms of angels who are neither married nor given in marriage. Reproduction is a consequence, at least to some extent, of the introduction of suffering and death.

The undoing of the consequences of the fall is best seen in Christ's deed on the cross. On dealing with the cause of the fall, in embracing God's will Christ in the flesh became Christ the immortal Man (the last Adam), rejoicing at the right hand of God. The undoing of the causes of the fall undid the consequences of the fall. Man, first of all in Christ, then took on the properties and attributes of the original created species known as man. He could again move in time and eternity with equal facility, as demonstrated by his meeting with the disciples on the Emmaus road after His resurrection. The same process (the reopening of paradise) is open to all who wish for it and seek it in the same way that Christ did.

The conclusion we draw then, as far as our original question is concerned, is that time and its concomitant decay, suffering and death were introduced to the whole of Adam's cosmos so as to permit a way back for Adam's cosmos. If Adam and his kingdom had remained in eternity, then Adam's sin would have remained forever frozen. Seen in this light, the tortures of our present time seem to be necessary mercies consistent with a God intent on restoring to man and his cosmos a kingdom of love, and intent on restoring to Adam His own image.

The undoing of creation was accompanied by the introduction of the second law and its concomitant death and decay. This is really the opposite of a creation and its concomitant decrease in entropy. The abolition of the second law, suffering and death, is in reality the same thing as re-creation and is spoken of as such in the Revelation of John.[26]

CHAPTER

7

Predestination and Free Will

No discussion of the implications of free will would ever be complete without mentioning the problem of predestination or free will. The whole subject is a difficult one and ought to be treated by a theologian rather than a mere scientist. However, this book has argued very heavily from the standpoint of free will, so it could be deemed biased, perhaps even tendentious, if we fail to mention that the so-called opposite doctrine of predestination or no free will does play an important role too. This was emphasized by Calvin, of course.

Can free will exist side by side with predestination or no free will without the two concepts mutually canceling one another out or producing nonsense? The Scriptures teach that they can and do exist side by side without annihilating one another. A comparison of a few texts, as set out in Table 1, will serve to confirm the above concept:

PASSAGES TEACHING FREE WILL

Thus it appears that the Scriptures do teach that man is able to say no to God, with all the temporal and eternal consequences of such an action. But the same comparison will also show that man is exhorted to say yes to God and can do so. Notice something new here. When a man has said yes to God he finds that he was predestined to do so. Man was not necessarily predestined to say no, although Judas was known prophetically as the son of perdition (foreknowledge). The point is, man is exhorted and wooed to say yes. But when he accepts the invitation he finds that he was predestined to do so and many more texts convey a similar meaning that God's eternal counsel had foreseen (not determined) the affirmative decision. In the case of Judas there was a foreknown no, and in the case of all Christians a predestined yes which emerges when they look back on their free will decision!

Passages Teaching Free Will	Passages Teaching Predestination
John 3:16	John 15:16, 19
Matthew 7:24, 10:32-33	John 13:1 8
Matthew 11:28, 12:50	Acts 3:17
Luke 6:47, 12:8	1 Corinthians 1:27
John 4:13, 11:26	Ephesians 1:4
John 12:46	2 Thessalonians 2:13

Such a position of free will existing happily side by side with plain predestination obviously cannot be handled by simple logic. From the ordinary human point of view one concept excludes the other. A paradox results. Having recognized this paradoxical situation, we must ask: Is reality (including the reality of free will or no free will) intrinsically paradoxical in itself, or is it our description of reality which is at fault?

To decide this point the following must be considered: reality is multidimensional and probably eternal, whereas we are three-dimensional and strictly temporal in our present state. Being temporal we use means of communication which are temporal and limited in scope. We are thus trying to describe a vast, apparently limitless scheme of reality in terms of a means of communication (language) which is highly restricted, limited, and generally inadequate for the great task demanded of it. To formulate reality, including that of free will and no free will, in our strictly limited means of description is like trying to describe a probability formula solely in terms of the Arabic digits $1=10$ with no algebra.

To illustrate further, light as we know it is a reality, a fact. Our eyes appreciate it without any difficulty at all. However, when we are asked to describe the reality of light by means of communication, we stumble upon untold difficulties. For we can, and do, describe light equally well either as corpuscular or as a wave function. It is, however, perfectly logical to say that if light is a wave function then it is certainly not corpuscular in nature. If it is corpuscular, then it is not a wave function. The one description excludes the other in terms of normal logic. Nevertheless, modern physics teaches that we must regard light as correctly described only in terms of both wave function and corpuscular concepts.

The area of real difficulty is now delineated: our dilemma with light does not lie in the reality and fact of light itself but in our attempted description of the reality of light in our means of communication. The complexities of light overload our descriptive possibilities, producing apparent paradoxes in the process.

We can try to overcome the apparent contradiction in our description of light by maintaining that light is either a wave function or a particle simply because it cannot in our logic be both at the same time. But if we cut out one description at the expense of the other apparently paradoxical one then we fall into overt error. For this one side of our description is inadequate in describing the reality known as light. The two antipodes are necessary to describe the whole of light. The real paradox lies then in our inadequate language rather than in the reality, light.

Returning to free will and no free will, if we were to maintain that the fact of free will cuts out the possibility of predestination or no free will simply because in our view the two concepts are mutually exclusive, then we commit the same type of error as we would if we maintained that light, being a wave function, cannot be corpuscular. If we go on to insist that free will is not capable of existing in the presence of predestination, we are committing the same error we have noted in parallel circumstances in light theory. The fact is that both free will and predestination express multidimensional reality. But we in our highly restricted view of reality cannot appreciate the fact that the two are congruent and not exclusive. To effect such a simplification is to introduce a false picture of reality.

Thus we maintain that free will is a reality and so is predestination. It is our limited means of description which makes them appear to be mutually exclusive. Reality contains both, and both describe reality. But we must note one important consequence of this. If free will is a reality in spite of predestination, then all the consequences of free will described in this book operate in full vigor—in spite of predestination which exists alongside it.

Thus I know that I of my own free will when confronted with Christ chose not to say no to Him. But having said yes to Him, I learned afterwards that my yes was, in the eternal counsel of God (ultimate reality) a foreknown and predestined yes. "No" is foreknown but, as far as I know, not predestined in the Bible. To eliminate either free will or predestination is to rob reality of one of its aspects which needs to be described by these terms. It is important to realize the difficulties of description with regard to infinity and eternity—phenomena with which our language and thinking apparatus both deal inadequately. But obviously for the purposes of this book the one aspect of the truth, that of free will, had to be emphasized to clarify the message. But it would be tendentious to try to eliminate the other side of the coin. If bonafide free will exists, as the Scriptures and experience maintain it does, then it exists in its full force and with all its consequences as outlined.

It will be obvious from the foregoing that if God courts man's free will decisions, He is aiming at influencing him for good.

This activity is entirely legitimate and does not interfere with our freedom of action.

The Scriptures teach that there is more in this question than merely influencing our wills for good. There is working against God's Holy Spirit also a contrary activity striving to influence man for evil. Just as a personal good One (God) courts our will for good, so a personal evil (Satan) courts us for ill. The Bible teaches that men do not fight only against flesh and blood in this life but also against spiritual wickedness in high places. The stark reality of this fact in the struggle for man's will and man's good is underestimated in this day when the masses of people really believe neither in God nor the devil. But a whole book would be necessary to attempt to deal adequately with this struggle.

BOOK THREE

Why Does God Allow It?

By A.E. Wilder-Smith

Contents

CHAPTER

1

A Baffling State of Affairs

"I can't understand it," the professor said to his colleague. "It is beyond my comprehension how otherwise intelligent people can say they believe in an all-knowing, all-loving, all-powerful God and actually refer to this God as a person. These people even imagine that they have a personal relationship with this personal, loving God.

"To a certain degree," he continued, "I can understand their attitude when they see a beautiful sunrise, an orchid in full bloom, or even healthy young men and women. But they must be very naive if they do not take a look at the other side of the coin. What do they have to say about the cat that sneaks to the mouse, plays with it, slowly tortures it, and finally devours it? Is this behavior nice, beautiful, and friendly? What about the young mother dying of cancer, her body stinking with decay before being laid in the coffin? Is that a sign and proof of God's great wisdom and love? And what about the horrors of war, especially those of today? Remember the gassing and other horrible methods used to kill God's 'chosen people'—the Jews—in the concentration camps?

"Why would a kind, loving, all-powerful God not only let such abominations happen, but as the almighty One, actually ordain them? Even godless people would have put an end to these atrocities if they had had enough power, but this "loving" God has let them continue for ages.

"Tell me what you really think about all the refined torture we see in nature around us. Take for example the process of malaria transmission. It shows signs of what looks like careful, well-devised planning, with the single purpose of plaguing and torturing its victim. To me, the whole system looks like a remarkable plan, as if both the good and the bad were planned for mankind and biology. As far as I can see, it appears that a Creator, if He does exist, is at the same time good and evil. An almighty and good God could not show so many evidences of what seem to be thoughtful, planned goodnesses in the universe and at the same time so many signs of calculated, cold-blooded sadism.

"Can anyone representing supreme wisdom and goodness also be terribly vindictive and evil, planning all sorts of plagues and tortures for men and animals? The whole concept is complete nonsense. And so is the idea of the wicked devil competing with God and single-handedly causing these difficulties. If God was almighty and good, He would have immediately extinguished the devil who then could not have clouded the issue. And if God is not able to prevent his devilry, then the devil must be equally powerful. We are then reduced to the primitive idea of warring gods in the heavens, an idea that has been erased through intellectual growth centuries ago.

"I used to say," he continued emphatically, "that I was an agnostic and therefore was not sure about these things. But now that I am older, I have come to the conclusion that in reality I am an atheist. I do not believe in a God, either good or bad. Such beliefs raise more difficulties than they remove, and just complicate the issue. Nowadays I avoid these considerations in my thinking; I do not need to darken my intellect any longer with such matters.

"May I also add that I cannot see how any intelligent, respectable person can believe otherwise!" The professor concluded his oration with a scowl that closed the door on any further discussion.

This man's ideas reflect the questions many people are asking today. If God is God then He must be almighty. Why then does He not bring all this chaos to a halt, all these wars, all the deception, injustice, misery, and disease in the world? If He loves us, as the Bible affirms, why does He not end all misery and produce order? If He were almighty, He could change everything immediately. He would no longer be God if He were not almighty, and if He is not that, why should we bother about Him? It is the concurrent existence of evil and good that has produced many atheists like the professor we previously quoted.

Why did God allow all of this? Does He no longer love us and care for us? Job asked the same kind of questions as the catastrophes befell him and his family. An all-powerful God could have prevented them—if He had wanted to. Did He then actually wish it to be so? Did He care about Job? If not, why should Job care about Him and continue to serve Him? Granted, there were still many things in Job's life that pointed to God's care in spite of thorns and thistles and family hardship, but there was no clear picture of God's love or care. Many signs existed for and against the existence of God's being, love, and care—just as they do today. One needs only to take a look at the world around him; the same contradictions arise now as then. Why should we believe and trust in a good God despite the evidence to the contrary? Some people say that the exercise of faith will eliminate this difficulty, but faith denies one of our highest faculties: the ability to weigh evidence and then to act on it. If the same Higher Being could plan both good and evil, beautiful and ugly, then all serious thought and human reasoning about Him becomes nonsense.

But before we continue, let us see what the Bible teaches about this state of affairs. Chapter 1 of the letter to the Romans clearly states that creation does not show the slightest sign of any of the above contradictions. Creation gives us only one line of thought that God is a glorious, omnipotent Creator and that His universe proclaims His almighty power. "Because that which may be known of God is manifest in them; for God has showed it unto them. For the invisible things of Him from the creation of the world are clearly seen, being understood by the things that are made (nature), even His eternal power and Godhead; so that they are without excuse" (Romans 1:19-20).

Thus the Bible teaches that if a man considers the universe and nature but does not at the same time see the power and being of the Godhead in them, then that man is "without excuse." It even goes one step further and teaches that the man who sees God in the image of His glorious creation but does not thank and praise Him for it—being overwhelmed with the wonders that reveal His wisdom—that man's thoughts will become "vain and his imprudent heart will become darkened" (Romans 1:21). This means that one cannot consider nature and the universe without being overcome with thanksgiving and worship toward the God who reveals Himself through it. And if one persists in refusing to see God in His universe, one will eventually become unable to use one's higher reasoning faculties and logical powers. One's heart will become darkened; one will become indifferent toward reason and morality. If mankind does not honor God upon observing His creation then man's logical ability will degenerate. Logic, says Paul in this portion of Scripture, demands thanks and worship to God. If refused, man's logical ability will perish!

We can see that the Holy Scripture does not show much sympathy for intellectual difficulties about believing in God. A glance at the present universe by a man of even minimal intelligence should be enough to convince him of the existence of a good and gracious God and bring about sincere gratitude and worship. How is it then that many intelligent people continue to run into intellectual difficulties which seem to make believing in God impossible? Investigation of that which is seen hasn't revealed to them the unseen, but has instead often turned them from believing in anything unseen at all! For what they have seen shows so many paradoxes that, judging the unseen by what they see, God becomes impossible, ridiculous, or superfluous for further serious thought. Atheism becomes the only solution they can accept without sacrificing their intellectual integrity.

CHAPTER

2

The Origin of Evil

Do the difficulties mentioned above really arise from the facts? Does the chaotic state of nature create insurmountable intellectual difficulties which stand in the way of one's belief in God? Perhaps a personal experience can clarify these questions.

Before the Second World War, I often visited the cathedral at Cologne. I admired this beautiful piece of Gothic architecture for hours at a time—its graceful flying buttresses, magnificent high-domed roof, medieval stained glass windows, and splendid organ. The more I admired the cathedral, the more I found myself admiring the architects and masons who had over the years designed and built the whole structure. Obviously the graceful lines had been carefully planned by experts possessing not only a knowledge of building mathematics but also an understanding of the principles behind beauty. The quality of their craftsmanship was first class in every way. My respect for these builders increased even more as I remembered that they possessed relatively few mechanical devices to facilitate their work. Thus the superb structure of that cathedral showed something of the superb minds behind it. It could not have come into being without enormous planning and preparation.

During World War II, Cologne suffered perhaps the most intensive air bombardment of any city in Western Europe. Since the cathedral stands almost directly in the railroad station yard (which was the target of frequent heavy bombing), it was often badly hit. I well remember the sadness of seeing the cathedral again in the fall of 1946. Practically every building near it had been razed to the ground, but high above the rubble the two famous towers were still standing. From a distance the towers still seemed to be intact, but upon coming closer one could see huge holes in the massive masonry. Hundreds of tons of concrete and bricks had been used to plug one huge hole high up on one tower, partially replacing the masonry which had been blasted away by an aerial bomb. The roof was a shambles, the organ was ruined, and everywhere lay knee-deep piles of indescribable rubble.

This miserable picture of chaos made a deep impression on me as I thought of the earlier order and beauty. While these memories were passing through my mind, I never once connected the current condition of this formerly beautiful building with any inefficiency on the part of the constructing architects or masons. Nor did I ever begin to doubt the existence of the architects merely because their handiwork lay before my eyes in shambles. Actually, the very rubble, the remnants of former beauty, showed how well the architects had planned the now-ruined structure. The mighty flying buttresses and the graceful Gothic arches were still there. Even the bombed-out holes in the walls made it obvious how well the architects had designed everything and how expertly the masons had built it. The bombs had laid bare their work, showing how well they had done their jobs. Thus even the very ruins were witness to the good architects' and masons' work! In some ways, the ruined structure showed even better than the intact one the perfection of the architects' plans and construction. There was no slipshod stucco or false walls such are found in many modern buildings.

Obviously no one could accuse the architects of having produced a ruin. In general, it is quite easy to distinguish between the ruined plan and the original plan. Although the cathedral displayed both perfection and ruin, order and chaos, it would be extremely illogical to conclude that there could have been no inventive mind or architect behind it, or that one could no longer hope to recognize any characteristics of the mind or minds behind it.

This bombed cathedral brings to mind the condition of creation today. It certainly is a hopelessly mixed picture of order and chaos, beauty and ugliness, love and hate, all inextricably mixed up with one another. But once again, it is illogical to assume that the edifice of creation has no mind or Creator behind it. This is the atheist position we mentioned above.

For the atheist maintains that he sees nothing but contradiction in nature. He therefore rejects from his world of ideas any thought of a Creator behind nature. However, we dare not forget that even the tiniest island of order in the largest sea of chaos demands a Creator of that small remaining order.

It is also a mistake to assume that because of the confused picture, no characteristics of a mind behind nature can be distinguished. In fact, one can often recognize design even better in a ruin than in the intact structure (as in the case of the ruined cathedral). The study of cancer cells (a good example of the ruination to which living entities can easily be reduced) has laid bare many secrets of the healthy, intact cell which otherwise would not have been so easily discovered.

Therefore, although creation presents a confused picture of good and evil, it is unreasonable to conclude that no Creator exists and that it cannot reflect His character. Destruction in creation often brings out the quality of the mind behind it better than its original perfect state does.

And yet atheists and agnostics maintain that a look at the world reveals nothing concerning the mind of a Creator, simply because of the hodgepodge of good and bad, the picture of order and disorder, which confuses the issue. Romans 1 teaches the untenable nature of just this thesis. For the apostle Paul maintains that illness, death, hate, and ugliness are all mere outward signs of an inward state of universal ruin. The outward signs of ruin are easily distinguished from those of health, life, love, and beauty, which still bear testimony to the original condition of things. Even the fallen creation reveals enough of the Maker behind it to bring any intellectually honest person to his knees in thankfulness and worship. For if he sees even the smallest island of love, order, or beauty in the largest sea of hate, disorder, and despair, he must acknowledge those islands with respect and worship for the One who created them.

CHAPTER

3

Why Does God Allow Evil?

Of course the illustrations which we have thus far used are incomplete. The illustration of the cathedral is no exception. Its incompleteness lies in the fact that the architects of the cathedral have long since died and could not have prevented the bombardment of their masterpiece. God is not dead, however, and the question arises as to why an almighty God who presumably loves His masterpiece (the creation), did not prevent its bombardment.

This then is the question: Why does a God of love allow all the evil and not put a stop to it? This question can only be answered by defining the nature of love.

215

One cannot adequately discuss God's love, of course, because He and His attributes are infinitely far beyond our ability to understand. All that is infinite lies outside the capacity of our very finite thinking apparatus. So we do not propose here to explore in any depth the question of God's love or virtue. We will consider love and virtue only so far as they deal with human love and virtue, and then we will apply what we learn to the indescribable phenomenon of God's love.

Although it is impossible for human beings to realize the extent of God's infinite love, the Bible teaches that we should try to understand as much as we can about it. To help us do this, He has illustrated His infinite love through an example of finite human love. The love of the Son of God, Jesus Christ, is for this reason often compared to the love between a human bridegroom and his bride. Christ characterizes Himself repeatedly as the bridegroom and His children as the bride.

In an attempt to understand God's love for us through the use of this illustration, we must pay particular attention to how love between a bride and her bridegroom originates. One day, the young man meets the girl and feels an attraction to her, an attraction better experienced than described. Traditionally, the young lady does not make the first move in this relationship but waits for the young man to do so. He begins to court her by sending her flowers or in some other suitable way. Before the courting really begins, the love affair is one-sided, and a truly one-sided relationship can be painful. The attentions must be returned if happiness and satisfaction to both parties are to result.

At this stage, there is one burning question which the young man would like answered: Is my attraction to her reciprocated?

The purpose of courtship is to settle just this one question. One fine day the young lady notices his attentions and attraction toward her and realizes that she must decide whether or not she is wiling to return his affection. If she is wise, she will consider this question carefully. She may seek the advice of her parents or a trusted girlfriend. Parents (and some friends) have had more experience in such matters than she. If she finally decides that she may safely return the affection, she must be sure that she can really love him totally and completely. If she can, an understanding may soon be reached between the two, and great is the joy of two hearts that have entrusted themselves to one another in mutual love, abandon, and faithfulness.

In order to better understand the process of falling in love, we must observe a few points. First, the young man must court the girl. If force or impatience take the place of courting, joy and love will cease. They are often replaced by hate and misery. The whole structure of love is built on mutual consent and total respect for each partner's character and freedom of will. In other words, the basis of human love is complete freedom to love—absolute free will on the part of both partners to either give or withhold their affection from one another. Without this freedom, true love is impossible.

When Eliezer, Abraham's servant, asked Rebekah to become Isaac's wife, he wanted to take her with him immediately after receiving the consent of her relatives. But the family knew it would be better if they discussed the matter with her personally. So they called a meeting of the whole clan, and only after she had expressed her own free will did they agree to the journey and the marriage (Gen. 24:56-58). This is the basis for love and marriage in all civilized lands. Both partners of a wedding must affirm their free will decision to marry and must individually answer, "I will."

Another important aspect of love involves the consequences of neglecting the above-mentioned mutual free will decision. The shocking love affair between Amnon and Tamar illustrates this matter (Sam. 2:13). Amnon fell madly in love with the king's beautiful daughter, Tamar, but just could not wait to woo her and win her love and consent. By deceit, he succeeded in getting her alone. In feigning sickness, he forced his "love" on her. The results of Amnon's brutal impatience was that his love turned in a flash to utter hatred toward her. Naturally, Tamar's heart was broken, and she remained desolate in her brother Absalom's house. The young girl suffered much more under this animal relationship than the young man did, which shows how necessary it is for men to understand that women are individuals to be respected and held inviolate.

The point here is that if love is replaced by force, then the possibility of real love is abolished and will be replaced by hate. Absolute free will, then, is a prerequisite of all true love.

The Bible teaches that God Himself is love. On this basis, He looks for a free willed responding love from us — a pure, warm, genuine love from the objects of His love. Love is only satisfied when returned; free willed love is won. God is not constrained in any way to love us, He just loves us because He is love. Such a divine love does not force us to return His love. The very attempt to do so would destroy the basis of all real love and all real virtue. As our true lover, God does everything possible to prove the genuine nature of His love, even to becoming a fellow man in the Person of Jesus Christ. Of His own free will, God (in Christ) died for us to free us from guilt and sin. God's Word says that greater love has no man than that which lays down a life for his friend (John 15:13). But Jesus Christ, as He courted man, went even further than this. He laid down His life for His enemies, thus demonstrating the greatest love of which man is capable.

Now consider one more vital point in our discussion of free will and love: What would have happened if God had so created man that he could not make a true free will decision for himself, but was capable only of automatically doing God's will ... just as a lock opens when one turns the correct key in it or as a vending machine delivers the bar of chocolate when the correct coin is inserted? If man had been so constructed that he delivered love and goodness whenever God pushed the right button, would he be capable of love or any other virtue? Could a system of real love have been produced in which man was so created that he was automatically virtuous, loving, kind, and incapable of sinning? Assume that God, in order to be sure of our love, had taken away our free will so that we could only love and never hate. He presses the button and we automatically deliver the goods — our love. Could such a creation in any way involve real love? If God had made us so that we could not hate, could we ever really love? The necessity for absolute free will in making decisions — to love or to hate — is inherent in any creation in which love and virtue are to exist.

Because God, being love, decided to create the possibility of true love among men, He had to take the chance that His intended partners in love would not love at all. God's eternal plan is to set up a kingdom of real love on earth and in heaven. But reaching this end involves a built-in risk—that of hate and vice arising instead of love and virtue. It is usually the person who has not considered this aspect of love who wants God to turn into a dictator and use brute force to forbid all of the evil that exists. But this person doesn't seem to realize that if He did, He would at the same time destroy all possibility of true love in our world.

Exactly the same risk is involved in planning any other virtue. Take, for example, the virtue of generosity. When a poor man begs for money to buy a meal, and I give him something, I am doing something good. On the other hand, when the city authorities send me a tax bill to help the poor and needy, it becomes my duty to pay. In this type of giving, I no longer exercise a virtue—even though the poor man may receive exactly the same amount of money he would have in the first instance. The difference is that in the first case I gave of my own free will. In the second, I paid taxes because it was my obligation to do so. Therein lies no virtue; forced charity is not charity at all, but a duty. This is the basic error of all socialist and communist plans to produce a paradise on earth. Their schemes are destined to produce vice, not virtue. If I force my children to be good when we are out visiting, they may be outwardly polite and well mannered, but I must recognize the fact that this goodness may not even be skin deep! Force itself can make no one good or virtuous. It may be very satisfactory punishment for wrongdoing, but in itself does not make anyone really good.

This thought discloses the weakness in our present social-ized world: most works of charity and works of love have been taken over by the State. Thus real works of love and true charity are abolished as soon as the basis of free will offering is removed. The socialist and communist state becomes a loveless, virtueless institution. The free will donater of money and goods obtains a blessedness or happiness through his voluntary giving. Jesus Himself remarked that it was more blessed to give than to receive. The exercise of any virtue ennobles and enriches the character, giving real joy and radiance to the one who exercises it. The taxpayer, on the other hand, pays his taxes because he must do so. In the modern state, being forced to pay taxes—even for charity—results in little happiness or enriching of the character. This is one of the basic reasons why life in a socialist state, which allows no freedom of action but controls every facet of life, generally robs its citizens of virtue and strength of character.

Many orphan homes throughout the world used to be supported and staffed completely by free will offerings and services. These homes full of young victims of suffering were real havens of love and joy to thousands of orphans. But nowadays many such private institutions have been taken over by the State and are supported by taxation. The result is often that the personnel of such institutions, instead of creating an atmosphere of love, are as cold and devoid of love as the concrete blocks of the walls which surround them. The welfare state, in taking over everything (in an attempt to remove some real abuses), too often kills real love and the other virtues which are dependent on freedom and which previously were the driving strength of the private institution. Of course, private institutions can be loveless too, but generally speaking, by removing the freedom of service on a voluntary basis, love and joy evaporate. This disastrous effect has been already imprinted onto the character of many modern nations and is nowhere more clearly seen than in totally socialized communities.

This absence of free will service paves the way to dictatorship, which has as a chief requirement lack of noble character in the mass of the citizenry. The strength of character necessary to withstand any tyrant is not likely to develop in any generation without the ennoblement of character resulting from long-term voluntary exercise of the various human virtues we have discussed. The modern socialized world tends to suppress just these character-building elements by adopting a false humanitarian attitude (free provision of every need from the cradle to the grave) in dealing with many of life's problems. A consequence of these facts is that even fewer men will possess the strength of character necessary to be ready and willing to suffer for conscience's sake in resisting the totalitarian demands of the socialist state.

When God created the celestial worlds and its angels, He planned on the very best; that is, a world of true love and virtue. To do this the very first requirement is, of course, complete freedom of choice for the inhabitants of that kingdom. Accordingly, the angels and their leader, Lucifer, were given natures capable of free choice between good and evil. Thus they were capable of genuine love toward their Creator and toward their fellows. They were capable of coveting His love and of being wooed by Him. This capability brought, of course, the corresponding possibility that they would reject God's love. The Bible reports that a large proportion of the angels followed Lucifer when he decided not to love and turned his back on his Creator's love. By rejecting the God of love, Lucifer and his angels became loveless—that is, hateful, envious, and vessels of all the vices which are opposed to the virtues summed up in God's character of love.

After Lucifer had made his decision against the God of all love, he began to seek companions for himself. Accordingly, he approached Adam and Eve, who were also capable of love and therefore possessed free choice. They, too, turned their backs on the God of love. They too became evil, introducing vice, sin, and suffering into man's realm; for to turn one's back on love and virtue is to turn one's face toward vice, greed, and hate.

Does the above not show the high esteem in which God holds His creatures? He takes our free will decisions and our love very seriously—seriously enough to court our love in good faith. Love always esteems and respects the freedom of its partner. This explains why God calls men by the method known as "the foolishness of preaching" and not by sending, as He could, mighty angels or superior intelligent creatures with His message. If they appeared in their supernal splendor, perhaps they would only succeed in terrifying humanity and fail to win men's hearts by a free will decision. God's real purpose is to win man's trust and love. For this reason, He uses natural, gentle methods to persuade us. He does not browbeat us with authoritative demonstrations. Such would be the method of a dictator, but not that of a lover. He employs no methods that would force mankind to accept His love, for one cannot terrorize people into love. The miracles that Jesus performed were designed with just this end in view—how often did Jesus forbid the recipient of a miracle of healing to publish the fact!

Thus we conclude that God allowed the universe to be bombarded because the plan was to establish a realm of free choice. The bombardment was merely the confrontation with a choice to do good or evil. Only in this way could a realm arise which was capable of genuine love and virtue. The construction of a kingdom of love, a kingdom of perfect freedom, involved the built-in risk of a kingdom of hell. Without this true possibility of a free will decision for heaven or hell, one can never establish the best — the perfect kingdom of love.

CHAPTER

4

God's Options

What could God do after His creatures had taken the bad road by turning their backs on the only good? What were the options left open to Him?

The Scriptures say that even before the wrong choice had been made by either man or angels, God—being omniscient—knew all about it and had even drawn up careful plans in advance to cope with the consequences. God's knowledge of the wrong choice and its consequences long before it took place has been a stumbling block to many. Actually, however, few intellectual difficulties are involved in this matter if it is carefully thought through.

If I observe a person attentively during a period of time, I may notice some of his little idiosyncrasies. He may say "ah," for example, as a prelude to every difficult word he has to pronounce. Or he may twitch his eyebrows before relating a good joke. Gradually on account of these observations, I learn to predict what he is going to do before he actually does it. However, my ability to foretell what he will do in no way makes me responsible for his actions. Similarly, the fact that God was able to foresee what Adam and Eve and mankind in general would do, does not necessarily make Him responsible for their actions—especially in view of the fact that He gave them the free will to act. God foresaw the fall of angels and men, and saw it so well that even before He had brought creation into being, He was prepared to send His Son as the sacrifice for wrong choice (sin). Yet many people imagine that God's foreknowledge of the fall must somehow make Him responsible for it. In fact, quite the contrary is the case. Man was given a truly free will, and with it came the possibility of real love and virtue or real hate and sin. This fact decides forever the creature's genuine guilt in the face of the Creator's love and righteousness in making him in His own image—that is, capable of independent choice and, like God, capable of real love.

At this point, the question may arise that if God saw in advance the chaos and awful possibilities of misery, hate, and suffering conferred on man with the gift of free will, why did He proceed to create us? Was He not rather sadistic to have persisted in those plans if He knew in advance the shocking results? Would it not have been better to have dropped the plan of creation before starting to create if it was going to work out as terribly as it has?

The same type of questioning arises every day in our own lives, as for example in our decision to get married. On the very day of our wedding, we know that one day the pain of separation from our partner through death is inevitable. We accept this future loss of joy because we believe that the present ennoblement of character in giving ourselves to the other in love even for just a single day is better than no love at all. In marrying we accept the utter misery of certain separation and death as the end of marriage, because we believe that one day of love and joy is worth more than the ultimate separation and misery at the end of marriage.

Evidently God also feels this way, because in order to have the possibility of some love, joy, and virtue, He accepted the accompanying certainty of hate and vice. It is a question of balance. Those who have known love will admit that it weighs infinitely more than the distress which its freedom may bring with it. Apparently the Creator, the God of love, agrees — for He went ahead with our creation in spite of the foreseeable mess which would result. He was convinced that the warmth of true love is worth infinitely more than the bitterness of suffering. Where life is, the opportunity to love exists too.

We shall escape the trials and sufferings of this life at death, but our character of love (ennobled through our trials) will continue to live forever. So whichever way we look we must admit that the creation — if it produced the possibility of love — is quite worthwhile, even if suffering may be involved. For love is the greatest of all virtues and far surpasses the misery which the freedom to love may entail.

Now that the fall has taken place and sin and anguish are in the world, what would we expect God to do? What does a Lover do who has been misunderstood and rejected by the object of his love? The Scriptures say that love "suffereth long and is kind, is not easily provoked, thinketh no evil ... beareth all things ... endureth all things ... never faileth" (1 Cor. 13:4-8). We expect true love to be longsuffering, kind, not easily provoked, enduring all things in the hope of the ultimate success of the wooing process of love.

God saw man's wrong choice which would lead to chaos and anguish long before the choice was made. When it did come, however, He did not disgustedly dismiss and destroy the object of His love as one might expect of someone treated unjustly. Instead, through loving patience He tried to salvage what He could out of the ruins. In faithfulness and sternness, He had warned of the consequences of the wrong choice, but He did not block the way back to Himself by attempting to force us to return. That would cut off all possibility of winning us back to love and thus defeat His main purpose in creating man — to insure a love relationship with Him. So He exercised longsuffering and patience in trying to win us freely back to love and reason. This process climaxed in the sending of His own Son to freely lay down His life for all of us. The Son went to His death so that love conditioned His death. Never once did He try to defend Himself, but, as He said, came to die freely for the sins of the world.

Even today He is patient with us, desiring that all men "come to the knowledge of the truth" (1 Tim. 2:4). Again in 2 Peter 3:9 His longing for us is emphasized: "The Lord is not slack concerning His promise, as some men count slackness, but He is longsuffering to us, not willing that any should perish, but that all should come to repentance." This means just what it says. It does not suggest that all men will repent, but that God is ready and willing to receive all who turn to Him and thereby reverse the effects of Adam and Eve's turning their backs on Him—the Source of all good. The man who chooses God is no longer subject to the sin nature he inherited from his first parents.

The fact that God has waited so long after the bombing of His handiwork before judging the bombers is yet another indication of His true character. It proves that He is indeed a God of lovingkindness, patience, longsuffering, and is not easily provoked. This is the only adequate explanation for the fact that God—the almighty, omniscient, righteous One—has not long ago exercised crushing judgment on all of us and set up a puppet state on earth and in heaven which automatically carries out His every command. Every dictator would certainly be anxious to set up such a totalitarian state, particularly if his will had been thwarted as God's will has been. But God's will might be even more abused if He did set up this puppet state to carry it out by force alone. Such dictatorial measures would effectively cancel the last small measure of love possible in this fallen creation. Those men who do see the situation as it really is and who therefore turn to God to be refreshed and regenerated by His love, find that even a little of such love and refreshment is better than none at all, which would be the case if freedom of choice—and therefore of love—were taken from us.

If the Lord had judged immediately after the fall (or any other sin), many who have since repented and turned to Him would have been lost to Him and His kingdom of love forever. Thus

His patience sees its reward in every sinner who turns to God in repentance and trust for renewal of virtue and joy, counteracting the vice and death induced by Adam's wrong choice.

A story is told about King George VI and how he won Elizabeth. As a young man, the future king of England fell in love with the pretty young lady from Scotland. After a time of reflection, he approached her on the subject of a closer relationship with her, but she refused him. (It is said that the prince had never been much of a lady's man and lacked robustness in his speech, appearance, and manners.)

Young George, greatly upset over this rebuff, asked his mother, Queen Mary, for her advice. She listened sympathetically to her son's tale of woe, and then told him she wanted to ask just one question before she could properly answer him. Did he really love only Elizabeth, or would he be able to consider a substitute if her refusal was final? After a moment's consideration, he replied that he wanted to marry Elizabeth and no one else. "Well then," said his mother, "there is only one way open to you. Go and ask her again." So the prince put his pride in his pocket, gathered up his remaining courage, and asked the lovely young Scottish lady again—only to be turned down once more.

After recovering from this second shock, he returned to his mother for counsel. Again she listened quietly, showing him every sympathy. But she asked once again if, after this refusal, he really did still love her. George was quite clear about his feelings. He loved her and desired only her among the choice of eligible young ladies. "In that case," said his mother, "there is only one option open to you. Go and ask her again."

After some time of mental preparation, the young prince visited the pretty young Scottish lady for the third time. She had, of course, noticed how serious the prince was; his love and determination to win her had indeed been constant. And she noticed something else. His consistent love for her was beginning to kindle an answering fire in her own heart. At last she was able to say that she loved him too and would like to become his wife. Thus the story goes, began a very happy family life that lasted until the king's death.

Love begets love, but love often has to be very patient, long-suffering, and kind until the fire is kindled in the prospective partner's heart. Once kindled, this love must be regularly tended in order to maintain the warmth of the blaze which God intends our love to be—warming and refreshing—so that both can rejoice in the happiness which love alone can bring. But it must be remembered that there comes a time in every love affair when the final answer to the lover must be given: either "yes" or "no." One day the courted lady may make a rejection which turns out to be a final. Not only has this lady a free will to accept or to reject the wooer, but the prospective bridegroom can also decide just how long he will continue to court and when he will desist. Even this final decision to desist will, no doubt, be made on the basis of love and will be postponed for as long as possible. But if the sought-after lady marries another, then the decision against any further courtship attempt must be made immediately. The Scriptures say that precisely this state of affairs may be reached in the spiritual sense when God's Spirit ceases to strive with a man or woman. Certainly God is reluctant to do this, and it hurts Him to have to give up on a man forever, but it is perfectly clear that this does occur—even though it is invisible to man's mortal eye. Jesus is the lover of man's soul, but there comes a time when man can irrevocably marry another. We can give our hearts entirely up to material matters, to social standing, to amassing a fortune, or otherwise to selling our souls—turning ourselves completely and finally away from the things of the kingdom of heaven. Then the days of courtship are forever over. The New Testament letter to the Hebrews speaks in several places of this fact (chapter 3:11, 6:46, 10:26-30). The advent of such days presents a gloomy picture and should serve as a serious warning lest we spurn God's grace.

CHAPTER

5

Epilogue

A consideration of the nature of evil and the nature of God's love leads us to believe that it is perfectly reasonable to believe in an all-powerful, loving God, in spite of the terrible state of affairs in the world He has created. If God is in fact love, and if He has revealed Himself as a perfect Man in Christ, we should actually expect the world to be in the position it is today. However, one can scarcely believe that God would allow His own creation to remain forever in its present state. He has promised to renew His whole creation and create a new earth and a new heaven where righteousness shall reign. In fact, the Bible teaches that those men and women who have tasted the bitterness and misery of making a wrong decision in turning their backs on Him can taste the love and joy of a right decision. Such will play a leading role in the renewed creation. It would seem to be less likely that they will once again make the same mistake and bring suffering into the renewed world by a repeated wrong choice. It is said that a burned child shies away from fire. A redeemed sinner shies away from sin. With those redeemed sinners, God will populate His new kingdom. At present, He is courting prospective candidates for the approaching new order on earth, which will be governed by Jesus Christ. This new creation will be ruled by the One who has proven Himself to be the best qualified for such a high office: the One who loves His creation (man) enough to die for him. Most rulers demand that their subjects show their faithfulness by their readiness to die for them. Christ, however, died of His own free will so that those He loves might live—forever. Certainly a kingdom founded on such principles will be well-managed and well-governed. "For He has made known to us in all wisdom and insight the mystery of His will, according to His purpose which He set forth in Christ as a plan for the fullness of time, to unite all things in Him, things in heaven and things on earth" (Eph. 1:9-10).

This plan for the fullness of time naturally refers to the reign of God's promised kingdom on earth as in heaven under Christ Himself. Everything in this kingdom will be summed up in Christ who will wield the power of attorney there. "Then I saw a new heaven and a new earth; for the first heaven and the first earth had passed away, and the sea was no more. And I saw the holy city, new Jerusalem, coming down out of heaven from God, prepared as a bride adorned for her husband and I heard a loud voice from the throne saying, 'Behold, the dwelling of

God is with men. He will dwell with them and they shall be His people, and God Himself will be with them; He will wipe away every tear from their eyes, and death shall be no more, neither shall there be mourning nor crying nor pain any more, for the former things have passed away'" (Rev. 21:1-4).

The participation of men in the coming kingdom has already begun here on earth for those who have allowed themselves to be saved from the present universal corruption and loveless-ness, trusting in Jesus Christ who has redeemed them from their sins. Our personal, individual choice for Christ today decides the issue of our eternal destiny—a kingdom of perfect freedom and perfect love between our Creator and ourselves. This is God's plan since before the beginning of time, and His love begs us to accept it. What will your choice be?

Notes

Book 1 / Chapter 3
1. cf P. Glansdorff, I. Prigogine, *Thermodynamic Theory of Structure, Stability, and Fluctuations in Wiley Intersceince*, John Wiley & Sons Ltd., London, New York, Sydney & Toronto, reprinted 1978
2. The results of the latest medical research into schizophrenia, cf *A singular solution for schizophrenia*, David Horrobin, New Scientist, 1980. Horrobin holds the opinion that schizophrenia may, among other factors, be linked with defects in prostaglanden-E-1-metabolism.

Book 1 / Chapter 4
1. cf A.E. Wilder-Smith: Der Mensch—ein Sprechender Computer, Schulte-Gerth-Verlag, Asslar, Germany, BRD, 1979.
2. cf A.E. Wilder Smith: Die Dimission des wissenschaftlichen Materialismus, Hanssler-Verlag, Neuhausen-Stuttgart

Book 1 / Chapter 5
1. F.H.C. Crick, *Thinking About the Brain*, p. 21, cf David H. Hubel, *"The Brain,"* Scientific American, 1979

Book 2 / Chapter 1
1. Rom. 1:19-20

Book 2 / Chapter 2
1. Julian Huxley, ed., *The Humanist Frame*, p.42
2. Acts 17:2, 18:4, 19, 24:25
3. Cited by Francis Schaeffer, p. 34. cf. Ps. 30:9-11

Book 2 / Chapter 3
1. A.E. Wilder-Smith, *Man's Origin, Man's Destiny,* Bethany Fellowship, Minneapolis, Minn. 55438, U.S.A. and, *The Creation of Life*, The Word For Today Publishers, Costa Mesa, Ca., 92628
2. Ibid.
3. Ibid.
4. *The Glorious Koran*, Dawood transl., Penguin Classics, New York, 1968. See also Prov. 16:6

Book 2 / Chapter 4
1. F. Schaeffer, p. 100
2. *The Glorious Koran*, p. 115, 167
3. John 3:16
4. R. A. Spitz, *The Psychoanalytic Study of the Child*, International Universities, New York, 1945, 1:53; 2:113
5. A.E. Wilder-Smith, *The Creation of Life*
6. 1 Cor. 1:21

Book 2 / Chapter 5
1. Heb. 12:2
2. C.S. Lewis, *A Grief Observed*, Seabury, New York, 1961, p. 25
3. 2 Cor. 4:17
4. 1 Cor. 13:4-8
5. 1 Tim. 2:4
6. 2 Pet. 3:9
7. John 1:9; Rom. 1:19-21
8. Prov. 8:31
9. John 3:16
10. Mat. 6:33
11. Heb. 3:7-11
12. Heb. 6:4-6
13. Heb. 10:26-31

Book 2 / Chapter 6
1. C.S. Lewis, p. 31
2. Acts 14:22
3. C.S. Lewis, p. 25
4. Ibid., p. 25-26
5. Ibid.
6. Mat. 27:46; cf. Mark 15:34; Ps. 22:1
7. Heb. 5:7-9
8. 1 Pet. 4:1
9. Mat. 10:24
10. Phil. 1:29
11. Mark 8:31, 9:12; Mat. 17:12; Luke 9:22, 17:25, 22:15, 24:26, 46; Acts 3:18, 9:16, 17:3; 1 Cor. 12:26; 2 Cor. 1:6, 4:17; Acts 26:23; 2 Tim. 2:12; Mat. 24:9; Col. 1:24; 1 Pet. 5:9; 2 Tim. 1:8; Heb. 11:25, 35; Phil. 3:10; Acts 14:22; Rom. 5:3, 8:35; Gal. 3:4; Phil. 1:29; 2 Thes. 1:5; Heb. 2:18, 5:8; 1 Pet. 2:19, 21, 3:17-18, 4:1, 19.
12. Phil. 3:7-11
13. 2 Tim. 2:11-12
14. Heb. 2:18
15. 1 Pet. 4:1-2
16. 1 Pet. 2:19
17. 1 Pet. 2:21
18. Luke 24:26
19. Luke 24:26
20. Acts 17:2-3
21. 2 Cor. 4:16-17
22. Rom. 5:3-5
23. Luke 13:4
24. Rev. 7:14
25. A.E. Wilder-Smith, *Man's Origin, Man's Destiny*
26. Rev. 21